THE FIRE AND THE

IRIS MURDOCH

The fire & the sun

WHY PLATO
BANISHED THE ARTISTS

Based upon the Romanes Lecture 1976

OXFORD UNIVERSITY PRESS

Oxford University Press, Walton Street, Oxford OX2 6DP

OXFORD LONDON GLASGOW NEW YORK
TORONTO MELBOURNE WELLINGTON CAPE TOWN
IBADAN NAIROBI DAR ES SALAAM
KUALA LUMPUR SINGAPORE JAKARTA HONG KONG TOKYO
DELHI BOMBAY CALCUTTA MADRAS KARACHI

First published in hardback 1977
Reprinted jointly as hardback and
Oxford University Press Paperback 1978

British Library Cataloguing in Publication Data

Murdoch, Iris
The fire and the sun.
1. Plato — Aesthetics
I. Title
700'.92'4   B398.A4

ISBN 0-19-824580-7 *Cased*
ISBN 0-19-283017-1 *Paperback*

Set by Hope Services, Wantage, and
Printed in Great Britain by
Richard Clay (The Chaucer Press), Limited, Bungay

TO JOHN BAYLEY

To begin with, of course, Plato did not banish all the artists or always suggest banishing any. In a memorable passage in the *Republic* (398 a) he says that should a dramatic poet attempt to visit the ideal state he would be politely escorted to the border. Elsewhere Plato is less polite, and in the *Laws* proposes a meticulous system of censorship. Scattered throughout his work, from the beginning to the end, there are harsh criticisms, and indeed sneers, directed against practitioners of the arts. This attitude is puzzling and seems to demand an explanation. However, what sounds like an interesting question may merit an uninteresting answer; and there are some fairly obvious answers to the question why Plato was so hostile to art. He speaks in the *Republic* (607 b) of 'an old quarrel between philosophy and poetry'. The poets had existed, as prophets and sages, long before the emergence of philosophers, and were the traditional purveyors of theological and cosmological information. Herodotus (ii.53) tells us that the Greeks knew little about the gods before Homer and Hesiod taught them; and Heraclitus (fr. 57) attacks Hesiod, whom he calls 'the teacher of most men', as a rival authority. Also of course any political theorist who is particularly concerned about social stability (as Plato, like Hobbes, had good reason to be) is likely to consider the uses of censorship. Artists are meddlers, independent and irresponsible critics; literary genres affect societies (*Republic* 424 c) and new styles of architecture bring changes of heart. A further and related possibility is that Plato simply did not value art (not all philosophers do); he sometimes calls it 'play', and if he thought it, however dangerous, essentially trivial, he would have less hesitation in harrassing it. Certainly the Greeks in general lacked our reverential conception of 'fine art', for which there is no separate term in Greek, the word *techné* covering art, craft, and skill.

However, after such considerations one is still uneasy. We,

or at any rate we until recently, have tended to regard art as a great spiritual treasury. Why did Plato, who had before him some of the best art ever created, think otherwise? He was impressed by the way in which artists can produce what they cannot account for (perhaps this suggested certain ideas to him), and although he sometimes, for instance in the *Apology* and the *Ion*, holds this against them, he does not always do so. He speaks more than once of the artist's inspiration as a kind of divine or holy madness from which we may receive great blessings and without which there is no good poetry (*Phaedrus* 244-5). Technique alone will not make a poet. Poets may intuitively understand things of the greatest importance (*Laws* 628 a), those who succeed without conscious thought are divinely gifted (*Meno* 99 d). And although, as the jokes in the *Protagoras* suggest, Plato thought poorly of literary critics ('Arguments about poetry remind me of provincial drinking parties', 347 c), he was obviously familiar with the most cultivated and even minute discussions of taste and literary evaluation. (Soup should be served with a wooden, not a golden, ladle. *Hippias Major* 291 a.) He even dubiously allows (*Republic* 607 d) that a defence of poetry might one day be made (as indeed it was by Aristotle) by a poetry-lover who was not a poet. Yet although Plato gives to beauty a crucial role in his philosophy, he practically defines it so as to exclude art, and constantly and emphatically accuses artists of moral weakness or even baseness. One is tempted to look for deeper reasons for such an attitude; and in doing so to try (like Plotinus and Schopenhauer) to uncover, in spite of Plato, some more exalted Platonic aesthetic in the dialogues. One might also ask the not uninteresting question whether Plato may not have been in some ways right to be so suspicious of art.

Plato pictures human life as a pilgrimage from appearance to reality. The intelligence, seeking satisfaction, moves from uncritical acceptance of sense experience and of conduct, to a more sophisticated and morally enlightened understanding. How this happens and what it means is explained by the

Theory of Forms. Aristotle (*Metaphysics* 987 a–b) represents the theory as having a double origin—in Socrates' search for moral definitions, and in Plato's early Heraclitean beliefs. He also (990 b) puts this in terms of the 'one over many' argument and the 'argument from the sciences'. How is it that many different things can share a common quality? How is it that although sensa are in a flux we can have *knowledge*, as opposed to mere opinion or belief? Further: what is virtue, how can we learn it and know it? The postulation of the Forms (Ideas) as changeless eternal non-sensible objects for the seeking mind was designed to answer these questions. It is characteristic of human reason to seek unity in multiplicity (*Phaedrus* 249 b). There must be things single and steady there for us to know, which are separate from the multifarious and shifting world of 'becoming'. These steady entities are guarantors equally of the unity and objectivity of morals and the reliability of knowledge. *Republic* 596 a tells us that there are Forms for all groups of things which have the same name; however, Plato only gradually interprets this large assertion. The earliest dialogues pose the problem of the one and the many in the guise of attempted definitions of moral qualities (courage, piety, temperance), and the first Forms to which we are introduced are moral ones, although very general non-moral Forms such as 'size' appear in the *Phaedo*. Later, mathematical and 'logical' Forms make their appearance, and at different times Forms of sensa are also admitted. The Form of Beauty is celebrated in the *Symposium* and the *Phaedrus*, and the Form of the Good appears in the *Republic* as an enlightening and creative first principle. (The light of the Good makes knowledge possible and also life.) In the *Phaedrus* and the *Phaedo* the Forms become part of an argument for the immortality of the soul. We are aware of the Forms, and so are able to enjoy discourse and knowledge, because our souls were before birth in a place where they were clearly *seen*: the doctrine of recollection or *anamnesis*. The incarnate soul tends to forget its vision, but can be reminded by suitable training or prompting. (The slave in the *Meno* is able to solve the geometrical problem.) The relation between the single Form and its many particulars or instances is explained variously, and never entirely satisfactorily, by metaphors of participation and imitation. On the whole, the early dialogues speak of a 'shared nature', and the later ones of imperfect copies of perfect originals. The use of the Forms in the doctrine and argument of *anamnesis* tends to impose a picture of entities entirely separated from the sensible world ('dwelling elsewhere') and this 'separation' is increasingly emphasized. (An aesthetic conception.) The pilgrimage which restores our knowledge of this real world is explained in the *Republic* by the images of the Sun and the quadripartite divided Line, and by the myth of the Cave (514). The prisoners in the Cave are at first chained to face the back wall where all they can see are shadows, cast by a fire which is behind them, of themselves and of objects which are carried between them and the fire. Later they manage to turn round and see the fire and the objects which cast the shadows. Later still they escape from the Cave, see the outside world in the light of the sun, and finally the sun itself. The sun represents the Form of the Good in whose light the truth is seen; it reveals the world, hitherto invisible, and is also a source of life.

There is of course a vast literature upon the interpretation of this myth, on the relation between 'the Line' and 'the Cave', and on how strictly we are to take the distinctions which Plato makes concerning the lower stages of the enlightening process. I shall take it that the Cave illuminates the Line, and that we are to attach importance to these distinctions. The details of what happens in the Cave are to be studied seriously; and the 'lower half' of the story is not just an explanatory image of the 'higher half', but is significant in itself. The pilgrim is thus seen as passing through different states of awareness whereby the higher reality is studied first in the form of shadows or images. These levels of awareness have (perhaps: Plato is not prepared to be too clear on this, 533 e, 534 a) objects with different degrees of reality; and to these awarenesses, each with its characteristic mode of desire, correspond different parts of the soul. The lowest part of the soul is egoistic, irrational, and deluded, the central part is aggressive and ambitious, the highest part is rational and good and knows the truth which lies beyond all images and hypotheses. The just man and the just society are in harmony under the direction of reason and goodness. This rational harmony also gives to the (indestructible) lower levels their best possible satisfaction. Art and the artist are condemned by Plato to exhibit the lowest and most irrational kind of awareness, *eikasia*, a state of vague image-ridden illusion; in terms of the Cave myth this is the condition of the prisoners who face the back wall and see only shadows cast by the fire. Plato does not actually say that the artist is in a state of *eikasia*, but he clearly implies it, and indeed his whole criticism of art extends and illuminates the conception of the shadow-bound consciousness.

I shall look first at Plato's view of art, and later at his theory of beauty. His view of art is most fully expounded in Books III and X of the *Republic*. The poets mislead us by portraying the gods as undignified and immoral. We must not let Aeschylus or Homer tell us that a god caused Niobe's sufferings, or that Achilles, whose mother after all was a goddess, dragged Hector's body behind his chariot or slaughtered the Trojan captives beside the funeral pyre of Patroclus. Neither should we be led to picture the gods as laughing. Poets, and also writers of children's stories, should help us to respect religion, to admire good people, and to see that crime does not pay. Music and the theatre should encourage stoical calmness, not boisterous uncontrolled emotion. We are infected by playing or enjoying a bad role. Art can do cumulative psychological harm in this way. Simple harmonious design, in architecture or in furniture, the products of wholesome craftsmanship enjoyed from childhood onward, can do us good by promoting harmony in our minds; but art is always bad for us in so far as it is mimetic or imitative. Take the case of the painter painting the bed. God creates the original Form or Idea of bed. (This is a picturesque argument: Plato nowhere else suggests that God makes the Forms, which are eternal.) The carpenter makes the bed we sleep upon. The painter copies this bed from one point of view. He is thus at three removes from reality. He does not understand the bed, he does not measure it, he could not make it. He evades the conflict between the apparent and the real which stirs the mind toward philosophy. Art naively or wilfully accepts appearances instead of questioning them. Similarly a writer who portrays a doctor does not possess a doctor's skill but simply 'imitates doctors' talk'. Nevertheless, because of the charm of their work such people are wrongly taken for authorities, and simple folk believe them. Surely any serious man would rather produce real things, such as beds or political activity, than unreal things which are mere reflections of reality. Art or imitation may be dismissed as 'play', but when artists imitate what is bad they are adding to the sum of badness in the world; and it is easier to copy a bad man than a good man, because the bad man is various and entertaining and extreme, while the good man is quiet and always the same. Artists are interested in what is base and complex, not in what is simple and good. They induce the better part of the soul to 'relax its guard'. Thus images of wickedness and excess may lead even good people to indulge secretly through art feelings which they would be ashamed to entertain in real life. We enjoy cruel jokes and bad taste in the theatre, then behave boorishly at home. Art both expresses and gratifies the lowest part of the soul, and feeds and enlivens base emotions which ought to be left to wither.

The ferocity of the attack is startling, though of course it is urbanely uttered. One can scarcely regard it as 'naive'. Nor is it surely (as Bosanquet suggested in *A History of Aesthetic*, Chapter III) intended as an ironic *reductio ad absurdum* ('if this is all art is, it's a failure'); though the deliberation is sometimes almost gleeful. Of course the Greeks lacked what Bosanquet calls the 'distinctively aesthetic standpoint', as presumably everyone did with apparent impunity until 1750, and this being so their attitude to art tended to be rather more moralistic than formalistic, and this is also true of Aristotle. Tolstoy exaggerates only slightly when he says (in *What is Art?*), 'the Greeks (just like everybody else always and everywhere) simply considered art (like everything else) good only when it served goodness'. Socrates offers it as obvious (*Republic* 400 e) that good writing and good rhythm and good design depend on good character. We might just entertain this as a hypothesis. The notion that tales which glorify bad men or art which stirs unworthy emotions may do moral damage is certainly familiar to us today, nor are we unaware of the social role of children's stories. The point about 'imitating doctors' talk' is also a shrewd one. The pseudo-authority of the writer (for instance the novelist) may indeed mislead the unwary. However, one is dismayed to learn that the censor is to remove one's favourite bits of Homer; and it may seem odd that Plato is unwilling to admire a clever imitation even as craft, unlike Homer who marvels at the verisimilitude of Achilles' shield at *Iliad* XVII. 584. (Bosanquet again, in search of Greek aesthetic attitudes. See *A History of Aesthetic*, Chapter II.) Moreover, to regard art as simple reduplication (like dull photography) seems to beg the whole question of what art is to an extent which seems to demand comment, even granted the lack of the 'aesthetic standpoint'. By contrast, Aristotle's remarks appear like luminous common sense. Surely art transforms, is creation rather than imitation, as Plato's own praise of the 'divine frenzy' must imply. To revert to the case of the bed, the painter can reveal far more than the 'one viewpoint' of the ordinary observer. The painter and the writer are not just copyists or even illusionists, but through some deeper vision of their subject-matter may become privileged truth-tellers. The tempting correction was made by Plotinus when he suggested that the artist does not copy the material object but copies the Form: a view which on examination turns out to be even more unsatisfactory.

Some of the views developed in the *Republic* are given a
trial run in the *Ion*, a dialogue regarded by scholars as very
early; the earliest, according to Wilamowitz. Socrates questions Ion, a rhapsode (poetry-reciter), who specializes in
Homer. Socrates wonders whether Ion's devotion to Homer
is based upon skilled knowledge (*techné*) or whether it is
merely intuitive or, as Socrates politely puts it, divinely
inspired. Ion lays claim to knowledge, but is dismayed when
Socrates asks him what Homeric matters he is expert on.
What, for instance, does he know of medicine, or sailing or
weaving or chariot-racing, all of which Homer describes? Ion
is forced to admit that here doctors, sailors, weavers, and
charioteers are the best judges of Homer's adequacy. Is there
then any Homeric subject on which Ion is really an expert?
With unspeakable charm Ion at least says, yes, generalship,
though he has not actually tried it of course: a conclusion
which Socrates does not pursue beyond the length of a little
sarcasm. Ion, though lightly handled by Socrates, is presen-
ted as both naive and something of a cynic, or sophist. He
may not know much about chariots but he does know how
to make an audience weep, and when he does so he laughs
to himself as he thinks of his fee. Socrates finally consoles
Ion by allowing that it must then be by divine inspiration
(θεία μοίρα) that he discerns the merits of the great poet. Plato
does not suggest in detail that Homer himself 'does not
know what he is talking about', although he speaks in general
terms of the poet as 'nimble, winged, and holy', and unable
to write unless he is out of his senses. He confines his attack
here to the secondary artist, the actor-critic; and in fact nowhere alleges that Homer made specific mistakes about
chariots (and so on). In the *Ion* Homer is treated with rever-
ence and described in a fine image as a great magnet which
conveys magnetic properties to what it touches. Through
this virtue the silly Ion is able to magnetize his clients. The
question is raised, however, of whether or how artists and
their critics need to possess genuine expert knowledge; and
it is indeed fair to ask a critic, with what sort of expertise

does he judge a poet to be great? Ion, looking for something to be expert on, might more fruitfully have answered: a general knowledge of human life, together of course with a technical knowledge of poetry. But Plato does not allow him to pursue this reasonable line. The humane judgement of the experienced literary man is excluded from consideration by Socrates' sharp distinction between technical knowledge and 'divine intuition'. The genius of the poet is left un-analysed under the heading of madness, and the ambiguous equation 'insanity—senseless intuition—divine insight' is left unresolved. It is significant that these questions, this distinction and equation, and the portrait of the artist as a sophist, make their appearance so early in Plato's work. Shelley translated this elegant and amusing dialogue. *He* did not mind its implications.

In the *Laws*, a treatise which describes a completely stable society, Plato pays the arts the compliment (and it is a compliment) which they now receive in Eastern Europe. Didactic uses of art are studied in detail; even children's games are to be controlled (797 b). Music and song are to be sanctified and rendered changeless, as in Egypt (657, 799), where the paintings and sculptures of ten thousand years ago are no better and no worse than those of today. The most impor-tant citizen in the state will be the Minister of Education (765 d). The Muses and the gods of games will help out fear, law, and argument (783 a), and the citizenry will be 'com-pelled to sing willingly, as it were' (670 d). People must be trained from earliest years to enjoy only good pleasures, and poets will be forced to explain that the just man is always happy (659 d, 660 e). The best literary paradigm for the writer to look to (this has the resonance of Kafka) is the book of the Laws itself (957 d). The *Laws* proves how seriously Plato took the power of the arts, but it adds little of relevant philosophical interest.

In the *Philebus*, however, one gets a glimpse of art in the context of beauty, and it is possible to construct a limited aesthetic out of materials found in this dialogue. The

Philebus, in which aesthetic imagery is freely used to describe the workings of the mind, is a discussion of pleasure. Plato has already (in the *Gorgias*) attacked the view that pleasure is the only good and has made known in earlier dialogues (especially in the *Republic*) his objections to gross or simple-minded hedonism. Greed, πλεονεξία, the violation of modest sense, is the typical fault of the pleasure-seeker. In fact Plato's conception of pleasure is, and must be, as we shall see, far more complex than these formal arguments, including that of the *Philebus*, suggest. It is agreed at the beginning of the dialogue that the good life must contain both pleasure and reason, the question being which of these makes it good. Pleasure is described as 'essentially unlimited' (31 a), and Philebus (who rarely speaks: some charming peevish boy no doubt) argues that it is its unlimited character which gives it its supreme value (27 e). Socrates, however, wants to connect goodness with limit, an idea which is associated with the Forms, here somewhat inconclusively present. Our human arrangements are a mixture of various sorts of un-limited material (τὸ ἄπειρον) with orderly limits which are imposed in the creation of the world by divine cosmic in-telligence (26). (The implication here is that these original mixtures are fundamentally good; that divine intelligence faces insoluble problems is admitted in the *Timaeus*.) We too bring about what is good by a right communion or associa-tion (ὀρθὴ κοινωνία) of the unlimited with rational limitation. The argument proceeds to suggest that only rationally controlled pleasures are good, and that intelli-gence, most kin to divine order, is the good-making ingre-dient in the good life. A distinction is made between true and false pleasures which is then carefully blended into a distinction between pure and impure pleasures (62–3). The clearer value of truth moves in to assist the obscurer value of good, and is joined in turn by the idea of the pure, always so dear to Plato. (The separated Forms are pure objects of spiritual vision.) Examples of impure pleasures would be those which are really a blend of pleasure and pain, depending upon physical contrast (cessation of discomfort) or upon mental contrast (envy, spite), or those which involve false judgements, where the falsity of the judgement infects the pleasure. Socrates says that some anti-hedonist thinkers have wished to argue that all pleasures are thus impure (false, bad); but he wishes to establish the existence of at last some pure pleasures. The first items upon his list are aesthetic. Quality of pleasure is here linked with quality of beauty. Some things are absolutely (truly, purely) beautiful, others only relatively so (depending upon falsity or contrast). Through sensation we pleasurably experience pure beauty when we see certain colours or simple geometrical figures or listen to single series of pure notes (51 c–d). Such pleasures are evidently never extreme or excessive. Beauty of animals (allowed at *Republic* 401 a) or of pictures is specifically excluded, and human beauty is not discussed. The list goes on to mention some pure non-aesthetic pleasures, such as smells (admitted to be 'less divine'), pleasures of learning (which are also lauded as attentive to reality, unlike fleeting contrast pleasures, at *Republic* 585), and certain pleasures connected with health and temperance and virtue generally (63 e) which are not described here, though they are bodied forth elsewhere in Plato's work. In fact the aesthetic examples, meagre as they are (and of course not intended as a formal 'aesthetic'), are designed to establish beauty in the crucial mediating role which it occupies in the dialogue. Socrates tries to 'save' pleasure by attaching it to reason and truth in the form of beauty, here narrowly defined through satisfaction in measure, moderation, and harmony. 'The power of good has fled away into the nature of the beautiful; for measure and proportion are everywhere connected with beauty and virtue' (64 e). Truth is pure and small in extent and not extreme (52 d), and pleasures which consort with truth and with the experience of beauty must be restrained and rational. Pleasure in general and apart from reason is the biggest imposter (ἀλαζονίστατον), and the greatest pleasures tend to be ridiculous and ugly (65 e). (Excessive pleasure and pain are said at *Timaeus* 86 a to be among the worst diseases of the mind.) Beauty enters the argument as something pleasant, but the dialogue ends with an attack upon the general conception of pleasure. Pleasure is by nature immoderate and indefinite and inimical to right proportion, and is thereby a prime cause of the breakdown in human affairs of the good compositions designed by the cosmic intelligence. Beauty is allowed only an extremely narrow connection with the pleasures of sense, though in so far as it is a proportion-bearing feature of the cosmos it is an aspect of Good, and as such properly attracts our love.

In reflections upon art it is never as easy as it might seem at first sight to separate aesthetic from non-aesthetic considerations. Much of what Plato says about art is concerned with the results of its consumption expressed in terms which are obviously moral or political rather than aesthetic. And even when it seems that he is clearly concerned with what is aesthetic ('contemplative') as opposed to what is grossly didactic ('practical'), it must be remembered that for him the aesthetic is the moral since it is of interest only in so far as it can provide therapy for the soul. The *Philebus* does appear to offer us, though with ulterior metaphysical intentions, an aesthetic method of judgement, though a very restricted one. There is nothing here about divine inspiration, except in the sober sense that it appears to be our duty to imitate the cosmic Mind. We should imitate only God, and that by sorting out and emphasizing and attending to harmonious patterns which are already latent in the universe. The area of acceptable art where pure pleasure, true beauty, and sense experience overlap is very small. Decent art must obey truth; and truth is expressive of reality (the two ideas blend in the word ἀλήθεια), and is pure, small in extent, and lacking in intensity. At 58 c philosophical truth is compared to a small piece of pure white colour. Art should thus take its humble quiet place in a life of virtuous moderation.

It may be said that Plato is a puritan and this is a puritanical aesthetic. Plato is of course a puritan; and doubtless had mixed feelings about the great artist inside himself. There is in all his work, and not only in the later dialogues, a recurring tone of sometimes almost vehement rejection of the joys of this world. Human life is not μέγα τι, anything much (*Republic* 486 a). The flesh is mortal trash (*Symposium* 211 e). We are shadows (*Meno* 100 a), chattels of the gods (*Phaedo* 62 b). Of course the Greeks in general always took a fairly grim view of the human situation, and the Pythagoreans regarded the body as a prison. But Plato's own austere observations have an unmistakably personal note. This is most evident of course in the *Laws* where we are told that men are sheep, slaves, puppets, scarcely real, possessions of the gods, lucky to be their toys. Human affairs are not serious, though they have to be taken seriously. We exist for the cosmos, not the cosmos for us. (644 b, 713 d, 803 b–c, 804 b, 902 b, 903 c.) ('You don't think much of men', says Megillus. 'Sorry, I was thinking about God', says the Athenian.) To be happy men must be abject (meek, lowly) before God (716 a). E.R. Dodds (*Greeks and the Irrational*, p. 215) comments upon this un-Greek use of the word ταπεινός, usually a term of abuse. Of course, by the time he wrote the *Laws* Plato had plenty of reasons for thinking poorly of mankind; but the tone suggests a religious attitude rather than a resentful one. God, not man, is the measure of all things (716 b).

It can certainly be argued that only simple, even naive, forms of art can be unambiguous companions of a thoroughly sober life. Like all puritans Plato hates the theatre. (And we can understand his feelings from as near to home as *Mansfield Park*.) The theatre is the great home of vulgarity: coarse buffoonery, histrionic emotion, slanderous ridicule such as Aristophanes directed against Socrates. Good taste is outraged by trendy showmanship, horrible naturalistic sound effects, and the raucous participation of the audience. (*Republic* 396 b, 397 a; *Laws*, 670 a, 700 e.) We are told in the *Philebus* (48) that the play-goer experiences impure emotion, φθόνος, spiteful pleasure, and delights in τὸ γελοῖον, the ludicrous, which is a kind of vice, in direct opposition to the Delphic precept; and such impure pleasure is characteristic not only of the theatre but of 'the whole tragedy and comedy of life' (50 b). In the *Laws* too (656 b) our easy-going amusement in the theatre is compared to the tolerance of a man who only playfully censures the habits of wicked people amongst whom he lives. The serious and the absurd have to be learnt together; but ludicrous theatrical buffoonery is fit only for foreigners and slaves: virtue is not comic (816 e). Words lead to deeds and we ought not to brutalize our minds by abusing and mocking other people (935 a). After the banishment of the dramatic poet in the *Republic* we are urged (398 b) to be content with 'the more austere and less amusing writer who would imitate the speech of the decent man'. Any gross or grotesque mockery would be regarded as a form of falsehood; and although Plato's work is full of jokes (even bafflingly so), one may sometimes get the impression that the good man (like the gods) never laughs. Plato is of course right in general (and his words are well worth our attention today) about the cheapening and brutalizing effect of an atmosphere where everything can be ridiculed. The question is also worth asking: what may I properly laugh at, even in my private thoughts?

The dangerous political role of the theatre would of course not be absent from Plato's mind. In the *Laws* (701 a) he deplores the 'vile theatrocracy' of an unruly auditorium. In all this there could even be an element of envy. (Plato often condemns envy; philosophers attack their own faults.) He had been himself a writer of poetry; and when a man with two talents chooses (or at any rate concentrates upon) one, he may look sourly upon the practitioners of the other. In the *Symposium* (176 e) Socrates congratulates Agathon upon his success in the theatre 'in the presence of thirty thousand Greeks'. ('You are being sarcastic', says Agathon.) No philosopher commanded such an audience, or would presumably wish for one; only philosophers are not always consistent. Plato often speaks bitterly about the lack of respect for philosophers and the inability of ordinary people to distinguish them from sophists. As a political realist (in the *Laws* for instance) Plato tolerates the theatre, but it pleases him to imagine a simple moderate life devoid of all such artificial nonsense. Consider the delightful, and surely not ironic, description in the *Republic* (372) of the small natural ideal state where men live modestly upon cheese and figs and olives, and recline garlanded drinking their wine upon couches of bryony and myrtle. Glaucon says, 'You are describing a city of pigs!' The arts do not make their appearance until Socrates sarcastically amends this picture for Glaucon's benefit. Greed damages societies and men. The best *technai* are those which remain modestly close to and 'co-operate with nature' (*Laws* 889 d), such as farming, physical training, simple cooking, and unfussy medicine. The *Timaeus* (88-9) recommends exercise and a natural regime rather than drugs; and the sensible carpenter (at *Republic* 406 d) who consults a doctor, accepts a simple immediate remedy but rightly has no time for elaborate treatment and so either recovers naturally or dies and is rid of his trouble.

The other aspect of the puritanical Plato is the passionate Plato. He commends homosexual love but says that it should be chaste, and in the *Laws* forbids homosexual practices. (*Laws* 836-7, 636 c; *Symposium* 210; *Phaedrus* 256 c.) He doubtless had his own experience of the divided soul. One may recall the sufferings of the bad horse in the *Phaedrus* (254 e) and the extreme and shameful pleasures mentioned in the *Philebus* (66 a) which are ugly and ridiculous and kept hidden in the hours of darkness. Of course much bad art deliberately and much good art incidentally is in league with lower manifestations of erotic love; therefore art must be purged. What art would the aesthetic of the *Philebus* allow the good state to possess? Plato's dictum that some colours and mathematical figures, imagined or bodied forth in objects (51 c), are absolutely beautiful and sources of pure pleasure is not on the face of it very clear. His words suggest entities too abstract or too simple to be able to hold the attention in the way usually associated with the experience of beauty. His frequent examples elsewhere may show us what he had in mind. Simple wholesome folk melodies would be acceptable, and certain straightforward kinds of military music. Plato was interested in music and in the Pythagorean discovery that the intervals of the scale could be expressed numerically. He often uses musical metaphors, and treats audible harmony as an edifying aspect of cosmic order (*Timaeus* 47 e). He takes the symbolic role of music for granted (for instance at *Republic* 400). However, perhaps because of the nature of Greek music, or because he feared its 'unlimited' expressive powers, he never seems to have been tempted to raise its status by regarding it as a branch of mathematics. (Other more recent censors have paid discriminating tribute to the importance of our emotional response to music, even while favouring this art because it seems void of ideas.) The pure colours envisaged by Plato would be wedded to simple mathematical patterns (that the forms would not be elaborate is made clear at 51 c), such as could appear on pottery, or on buildings which could themselves be plainly designed objects of beauty, or upon the embroideries of which Plato more than once speaks. Above all the spirit of the work must be modest and unpretentious. The paintings of (for instance) Mondrian and Ben Nicholson, which might be thought of as meeting his requirements, would I think be regarded by Plato as histrionic and danger-ously sophisticated. All representation would of course be barred. In general, folk art and simple handicrafts would express the aesthetic satisfactions of his ideal people. The didactic poetry permitted by the *Republic* and the *Laws* ('hymns to the gods and praises of good men') would be justified by its effective operation upon the soul, although it might no doubt promote a pleasure less than pure.

We may pause here for a moment and compare Plato's views, as expressed in the *Philebus*, with those of two other great puritans, Tolstoy and Kant. Plato's fear of art, and theirs too, is to some extent a fear of pleasure. For Tolstoy, art should be defined not through the pleasure it may give, but through the purpose it may serve. Beauty is connected with pleasure, art is properly connected with religion, its function being to communicate the highest religious perceptions of the age. The kind of art which Tolstoy particularly disliked (and which he freely criticized by the 'can't make head or tail of this stuff' method), the inward-looking art-fostered art of the later Romantics (Baudelaire, Mallarmé, Verlaine), is deliberately obscure and 'the feelings which the poet transmits are evil'. Tolstoy also condemned Shakespeare for lack of moral clarity. Elaborate art tends to be a kind of lying. Tolstoy would agree with *Philebus* 52 d: intensity and bulk are not connected with truth. Academic aesthetic theories are pernicious because they present art as some sort of complex lofty mystery. But there is no mystery. Purity, simplicity, truthfulness, and the absence of pretence or pretention are the marks of sound art, and such art is universally understood, as are simple folk tales and moral stories. Ordinary people know instinctively that art becomes degraded unless it is kept simple. By these criteria Tolstoy was quite prepared to dismiss almost all his own work as bad. (He excepted *A Prisoner of the Caucasus* and *God Sees the Truth and Waits. What is Art?*, Chapter VI.) Tolstoy particularly detested opera. Plato would have detested it too. Complex or 'grand' art affects us in ways we do not understand, and even the artist has no insight into his own activity, as Socrates says with sympathetic interest in the *Apology* and airy ridicule in the *Ion*.

Both Plato and Kant, because they are so well aware of the frightful devious egoism of the human soul, are anxious to build metaphysical barriers across certain well-worn tracks into depravity; and to keep apart certain ideas which are longing to merge. Kant's almost fanatical insistence on strict truthfulness has its counterpart in Plato, only this is to some extent obscured by Plato's artful playfulness. Plato wants to cut art off from beauty, because he regards beauty as too serious a matter to be commandeered by art. He allows morality to enter art but only at a simple level (as a reminder of higher harmonies) or under the eye of the censor. Kant, on the other hand, wants to cut beauty off from morals. Kant restricts beauty for the same reason for which Plato restricts art, to get it cleanly out of the way of something more important.

Plato constantly uses the image of the harmonious whole which determines the proper order of its parts. This indeed is one of his prime images. The soul, the state, the cosmos, are such organic wholes; and he speaks (for instance at *Phaedrus* 286 d) of the way in which inspired imagination goes beyond technique in art to produce a kind of completeness. But whereas Aristotle discusses aesthetic structure in terms entirely familiar to us (*Poetics* VII, VIII: 'A whole is what has a beginning, a middle and an end.' 'That whose presence or absence makes no perceptible difference is not an integral part of the whole'), Plato never sets up any such definition of our 'work or art', nor indeed does he, except ostensively, define art as opposed to craft. He tends to discuss the effects of styles and patterns rather than the nature of complete objects. We think of art primarily as objects, but there are whole art traditions, notably that of Islam, which do not. Kant does offer a definition, when he describes beauty as coming about when the imagination composes sense experience under the general, orderly, object-forming guidance of the understanding, but without a concept. Beauty has an objective formal occasion, but is a unique subjective composition with an air of purposeful organization, but no purpose. In the *Critique of Judgement* Kant offers two accounts of beauty. One is narrow and formalistic (as it were what beauty ought to be like); the other, taking more account of actual works of art, and developing the idea of the artist as the inspired 'genius', is wider and more confused. (Genius does not know its method.) Almost all 'real' art turns out to be 'impure'; Kant would certainly agree with Plato that the pleasures of literature are. In the stricter account the pure judgement of taste bears upon formal properties only; desire, charm, or moral or intellectual content are excluded. Colour is merely charming. Geometrical figures as such are not beautiful because they are constituted by a concept. Kant's examples of pure conceptless beauty, in art or nature, have a Platonic simplicity: birds, flowers (tulips for instance, of which Kant appears to have been fond), Greek-style designs, patterns of foliage on wallpaper. (Plato would not have objected to unpretentious wallpaper.) Though pure beauty has no moral message, the instinctive enjoyment of natural beauty is the mark of a good soul: the forms of natural beauty are spiritually superior to those of art.

Plato distinguishes between very simple permissible beauty in art, and beauty in nature which, as I shall explain, he regards as very important. Kant admits pure beauty in nature only at levels of satisfaction in simple forms, such as leaves and flowers. Beauty in nature is always in danger of becoming merely charming: the song of the nightingale conjures up the 'dear little bird', and is spoilt for us if we are then told that it is produced by a boy hidden in the grove. The wilder aspects of nature have for him a higher role to play. In distinguishing the sublime from the beautiful, Kant gears his whole machine to the attempt to keep the claims of the spiritual world quite separate from the simpler more egoistic and undemanding enjoyment of beauty. We apprehend beauty and rest in the contemplation thereof when sense experience inspires the imagination to formulate some unique non-conceptual pattern. The sublime, on the other hand, is a disturbing feeling (which we regard as an attribute of its cause) which arises in us when reason's authoritative demand for intelligible unity is defeated by the formless vastness or the power of nature; its aspect as 'unlimited', to use the language of the *Philebus*: the starry heavens, mountains, waterfalls, the sea. It is a kind of aesthetic and yet moral feeling of mixed pleasure and pain, akin to the respect which the moral law inspires: pain at reason's defeat, but pleasure at our responding sense of reason's dignity and spiritual value. The sublime stirs and wakens our spiritual nature. In this experience we are not led into theoretical studies of natural form, but receive a shock from nature's lack of form, and our inspiriting pleasure is a pure product of our moral faculty. The sublime, not the beautiful, connects us through purified emotion with the highest good and is an active agent of enlightenment. This metaphysical separation, insisted on by Kant, is inimical both to common sense egoism (which rejects the sublime or treats it as beautiful) and to Hegelian idealism (which demands the reduction of the two areas to intelligible unity). Thus for instance Bosanquet: 'With Turner and Ruskin before us we do not comprehend the aesthetic perception to which, as to Kant, the stormy sea was simply horrible' (*History of Aesthetic*, Chapter X). This evades Kant's whole point; and the Romantic movement shockingly cheated him in taking over the sublime. Kant is attempting, as Plato is, clearly and finally to separate unresting spiritual aspiration from a restful satisfaction in the pleasing forms of art or nature. Plato too gives nature a stirring spiritual role, only here it is nature as beautiful which awakes the dreaming captives. Plato is of course indifferent to many of the show-pieces of the Kantian sublime (mountains, sea) as well as to the more ordinary charms of nature. Socrates says in the *Phaedrus* (230 d) that fields and trees have nothing to teach him. Plato would agree with Kant about the edifying role of the starry heavens; only Kant would be edified by reason's defeat (theoretical studies do not thus enlighten us), whereas for Plato the stars would properly inspire us to geometry (*Republic* 530 a), thus to philosophy (*Timaeus* 47 c) shining as evidence of a divine hand, endowed with souls (*Timaeus* 41 e), or as visible gods (*Laws* 899 b). 'Can we then deny that everything is full of gods?' Plato asks here, quoting Thales.

Plato temperamentally resembles Kant in combining a great sense of human possibility with a great sense of human worthlessness. Kant is concerned both with setting limits to reason, and with increasing our confidence in reason within those limits. Though he knows how passionate and how bad we are, Kant is a moral democrat expecting every rational being to be able to do his duty. Plato, on the other hand, is a moral aristocrat, and in this respect a puritan of a different type, who regards most of us as pretty irrevocably plunged in illusion. Plato (except mythically in the *Timaeus*) sets no theoretical limits to reason, but the vast distance which he establishes between the good and the bad makes him as alien to Hegel as Kant is. Plato is accused of moral 'intellectualism', the view that we are saved not by ordinary morality but somehow by thinking. Let us now look more closely at what Plato considered thinking to be like. He was concerned throughout with how people can change their lives so as to become good. The best, though not the only, method for this change is *dialectic*, that is, philosophy regarded as a spiritual discipline. The aim of Socrates was to prove to people that they were ignorant, thus administering an intellectual and moral shock. In the *Sophist* (230 c), dialectic is described as a purgation of the soul by ἔλεγχος, argument, refutation, cross-questioning; and in the *Phaedo* (67 e) true philosophers are said to 'practise dying'. Philosophy is a training for death, when the soul will exist without the body. It attempts by argument and the meticulous pursuit of truth to detach the soul from material and egoistic goals and enliven its spiritual faculty, which is intelligent and akin to the good. Now what exactly is philosophy? Some might say that philosophy is certain arguments in certain books, but for Plato (as indeed for many present-day philosophers) philosophy is essentially talk. *Viva voce* philosophical discussion (the ψιλοὶ λόγοι of *Theaetetus* 165 a) is the purest human activity and the best vehicle of truth. Plato *wrote* with misgivings, because he knew that truth must live in present consciousness and cannot live anywhere else. He expressed these misgivings in the *Phaedrus* and (if he wrote it) in the *Seventh Letter*.

The remarks about writing in the *Phaedrus* are very striking and cannot but have relevance to Plato's view of art, not only because some writing is art. Of course in Plato's time books were still rather rare luxury articles. Phaedrus says (257 d) that many people hesitate to leave written speeches behind them for fear of being called sophists. Socrates (274-5) proceeds to explore the propriety or impropriety of writing by means of a myth. Theuth (Thoth, alias Hermes, also mentioned in the *Philebus*), a deity living in Upper Egypt, whom Plato here credits with the invention of number, arithmetic, geometry, astronomy, draughts, and dice, comes to Thamous, who is King and God, and says: 'My lord, I have invented this ingenious thing, it is called *writing*, and it will improve both the wisdom and the memory of the Egyptians.' Thamous (God is always doing geometry, but he cannot write) replies that, on the contrary, writing is an inferior substitute for memory and live understanding. Men will be led to think that wisdom resides in writings, whereas wisdom must be in the mind. A book cannot answer back or distinguish wise or foolish readers. (Plato expresses this view as early as *Protagoras* 329 a.) It needs its parent to speak for it. Like a painting, it says always one thing and cannot explain. The gardens of literature produce ephemeral flowers, for amusement only. The wise man will plant in suitable souls seeds which are not sterile, when properly understood thought is conveyed in live discussion. ('How easily you make up stories from Egypt or any country you please!' says Phaedrus admiringly. 'In the past, dear boy,' says Socrates, 'people were content to listen to an oak or a rock provided it spoke the truth.') Only words inscribed on the soul of the hearer enable him to learn truth and goodness; such spoken truths are a man's legitimate sons. Writing spoils the direct relationship to truth in the present. Since truth (relation to the timeless) exists for incarnate beings only in immediate consciousness, in live dialectic, writing is precisely a way of absenting oneself from truth and reality. The *Seventh Letter* makes the same point even more emphatically. What is really important in philosophy cannot be put into written words and scarcely indeed into words. (Language itself may be a barrier.) Written words are the helpless victims of men's ill will, and encourage inferior exposition at second hand. Writing can easily become a kind of lying, something frivolously pursued for its own sake, in fact an art form. True understanding comes suddenly to trained thinkers after sustained and persistent discussion; and there is little danger of a man forgetting the truth once he has grasped it since it lies within a small compass.

The spirit of this tirade is curiously contemporary, and may remind us of familiar existentialist arguments and their more recent offspring in the form of attacks upon literacy and art, mounted by literate people and artists. These demonstrations, even at their least serious or most naive, are conceived in the interests of truth, which here appears variously in the guises of sincerity, genuine feeling, freedom, and so on. A truer heir of Plato's argument is to be found within philosophy in the form of an attack upon system, jargon, grandeur, and the development of wordy theories which prevent a simple lively relationship with truth. (The dialogue form itself is of course a slight precaution against monolithic system.) Modern thinkers as unlike each other as Kierkegaard and Wittgenstein have felt acutely what Plato gives expression to. Kierkegaard, fighting Hegel, attempted to use art itself as an anti-theoretical mystification in order to scare off disciples and promote live thought. Wittgenstein scared disciples by the direct method and also wrote with reluctance because he feared that his books would fall into the hands of fools. He too thought that there was little danger of forgetting what had once been properly understood. Criticizing some of his own work he is reported as saying in conversation: 'No. If this were philosophy you could learn it by heart.' What has been clearly seen is appropriated and cannot be lost.

It is necessary before discussing this further to fill in some metaphysical background to it. Writing, invented by the god who invented numbers and games, so sadly remote from reality, may be viewed as a case of an even more general Platonic problem. Here we must look for a moment first at the doctrine of *anamnesis* (recollection), and then at the adventures and misadventures of the Theory of Forms. Plato asks the question, which so many philosophers have asked since (Hume and Kant asked it with passion): how do we seem to know so much upon the basis of so little? We know about perfect goodness and the slave in the *Meno* knows geometry because the soul was once separate from the body (and will presumably be so again) and saw these things clearly for itself. Learning is recollection (*Phaedo* 91 e). Now when incarnate it is confused by ordinary sense perception, but can gain some refreshment from the contemplation of eternal objects to which it is akin and which it feels prompted to rediscover; although of course (*Phaedo* 66) such contemplation must always be imperfect so long as the soul and the body remain together.

The idea of unconscious knowledge goes very far back in Plato and was in some original form no doubt adopted by him from those (Pythagoreans) mentioned at *Phaedo* 62 b who held that the soul is imprisoned in the body and has a home elsewhere to which it goes and from which it returns. The divinely inspired prophet was of course in Greece (as elsewhere) a familiar figure, the man who mysteriously knows more than he can explain or understand. The human mind is potentially connected with an obscure elsewhere; and traditionally the poets, as inspired beings, could also count as seers. The Muses are after all the daughters of Memory, and Apollo (*Cratylus* 405 a) is both prophet and musician. Prophetic and poetic madness are juxtaposed in the *Phaedrus*. Plato was clearly fascinated by the unconscious nature of the artist's inspiration, which he constantly mocks, but which he also uses as a clue. In the *Protagoras* (347 e) he prefers the company of philosophers to that of poets, since poets never know what they are talking about, and neither does anybody else. In the *Meno*, however, he asks: can virtue be taught? No, not even by Themistocles or Aristides or Pericles. Some things are teachable (διδακτόν), others must be 'remembered' (ἀναμνηστόν, 87 b). Even statesmen who are wise are like the poets in that they do not know the source of their wisdom.

Plato concludes that wisdom comes to us somehow 'by divine dispensation' (θεία μοίρα, 100 b). There is indeed no limit to the power of remembering since 'all nature is akin and the soul has learnt everything' (81 d), so through recovering one thing we can by this mysterious process go on to recover others. The creative mind instinctively connects, and a profound idea joins the far-fetched to the familiar and illuminates its own evidence. Plato (for instance) at *Republic* 572 a tells of soothing anger by deliberately falling asleep with quiet thoughts; and the discussion of education in the *Laws* shows how much he had reflected upon the powers of 'subliminal' persuasion.

The world rediscovered in *anamnesis* is the world of the Forms, and the Forms have in Plato's thought a history which is both complex and obscure. The most beautiful vision of the Forms as objects of veneration and love is given to us in the *Phaedrus* (250) where (in a myth) they are referred to as 'realities' or 'entities' (ὄντα), quasi-things which can be seen as passing in procession. They are seen 'by the soul alone' when it seeks 'by itself' (*Phaedo* 66 d, 79 d), and are therefore associated with the hope of the soul's immortality. The Form of Beauty (*Symposium* 211) shines forth by and in itself, singular and eternal, whereas the Forms 'with us' are infected and fallen 'trash'. The 'lovers of sights and sounds', including connoisseurs of art, at *Republic* 476 are 'dreaming' because they take a resemblance for a reality. One does not have to read far in Plato to see that the Aristotelian explanation of the origin of the Theory of Forms in terms of 'logic' is only part of the picture. From the start the need for the Forms in Plato's mind is a moral need. The theory expresses a certainty that goodness is something indubitably real, unitary, and (somehow) simple, not fully expressed in the sensible world, therefore living elsewhere. The eloquence and power of Plato's evocation may in itself persuade us, in particular contexts, that we understand, but of course it is never very easy to see what the Forms are supposed to be, since in speaking of them

Plato moves continually between ontology, logic, and religious myth. F. M. Cornford argues that when the theory first appears 'the process of differentiating concepts from souls has not yet gone very far in Plato's mind' (*From Religion to Philosophy*, section 132). On this view the Form was originally conceived as a piece of soul-stuff or a daemonic group-soul. It is scarcely possible to develop any such idea with precision; Plato speaks of the Forms with a remarkable combination of absolute confidence and careful ambiguity. In so far as the historical Socrates was interested in studying moral concepts it might seem that the first Forms were definitions or (in the modern sense) universals. Yet the tendency to reify them also begins early. The Form represents the *definiendum* as it is 'in itself' (αὐτὸ καθ' αὐτό); and *Protagoras* 330 c even tells us that Justice is just. The early Forms also 'participate' in particulars and thus give them definition and some degree of reality. But from the *Phaedo* onward Plato develops, especially in moral and religious contexts, a picture of the Forms as changeless and eternal and *separate* objects of spiritual vision known by direct acquaintance rather than through the use of language (propositions). The mediocre life is a life of illusion. The discovery of truth and reality, the conversion to virtue, is through the unimpeded vision of the transcendent Forms. At the same time, in his more logical metaphysical contexts, Plato criticizes and even attacks this picture, without however abandoning it; it reappears in a splendid mythological guise in the *Timaeus*, and evidently expresses something for which Plato cannot find any other formulation. The last reference to the Forms is the sober one at *Laws* 965. 'Can there be any more accurate vision or view of any object than through the ability to look from the dissimilar many to the single idea?' Here the language of vision seems plainly metaphorical. A mysterious late unwritten doctrine is said to associate the Forms with numbers (the Good is the One), but of this little can be said. Plato played in many ways with the concepts of one, many, limit, and it seems unlikely that the 'number' doctrine represents anything entirely new. Dialectic (philosophy) follows the varying fates of the Forms, thus appearing sometimes as mystical vision, sometimes as meticulous classification, the ability to make distinctions and discern relevant differences (*Politicus* 285a, *Philebus* 16–17).

The most radical doubts concerning the reified or visionary Forms occur in the *Parmenides*, *Theaetetus*, and *Sophist*. In the *Parmenides* the youthful Socrates attempts to expound a doctrine of Forms which is subjected to damaging criticism by Parmenides. No sense can be made of the idea of 'participation', the relation between a particular and a 'similar' Form leads to a vicious regress (the 'third man' argument), and it is in general impossible to establish how Forms can be known. Parmenides also presses upon Socrates the question: what are there Forms of? The theory has thriven upon a consideration of the great moral Forms, the mathematical Forms of the *Republic*, and certain other respectable Forms of great generality. But are there Forms of everything, even of trivial things such as mud, hair, and dirt? (As *Republic* 596a, where Forms are associated with common names, would suggest.) When Socrates inclines to say no, Parmenides rightly points out that if he gives up here he is not yet a philosopher. At the same time, and in spite of his criticisms and questions, Parmenides holds that (somehow) Forms are necessary for knowledge and discourse, since 'you must always mean the same thing by the same name' (147d). The *Theaetetus* does not refer directly to the Forms, though certain important 'common qualities' are discussed (185c). The dialogue mainly concerns the absolute difference between knowledge and opinion, which was an original founding idea of the theory. In discussing the quarrel between the followers of Parmenides and of Heraclitus (the One men and the flux men) Socrates, rejecting 'total motion' and 'total rest', anticipates the arguments of the *Sophist*; and we are told at 182b that nothing is one 'all by itself' (αὐτὸ καθ᾽ αὐτό). 'False opinion' is considered (how is it that we make mistaken judgements?), and there is a long and inconclusive attempt to define 'knowledge'. The argument rejects the view that knowledge is perception (the evident presence of the known where the mind 'touches' it) or that it is true opinion, or true opinion with an explanation (*logos*) attached; the ability to distinguish particulars always involves more insight into relevant differences than can be unambiguously expressed, so the particulars lie inaccessibly under the net of the mode of expression.

The *Sophist* (where Theaetetus is questioned by a visiting follower of Parmenides and Zeno) returns to the Forms and picks up problems left unsolved in the *Parmenides* and the *Theaetetus*. What is knowledge? What are negation and falsehood? How is it that the Forms are essential to thought? How does Being enter Becoming, how can it? Plato also makes an important move in allowing (248) that what knows (soul, ψύχη) must be as real as what is known (Forms). This leaves the way open for the *Timaeus* and for the much enhanced role of ψύχη in that dialogue and in the *Laws*, where real truth-knowing Soul appears as a mediator between changeless being and the world of sense, whose status as real is from now on quietly upgraded. Being must accommodate both motion and rest; and Plato here concedes the necessity of a theory of motion as part of a theory of the real, and thus comes closer to the scientific interests of his predecessors, interests which he himself pursues in the *Timaeus*. The formal pretext of the *Sophist* is the use of the dialectical method of 'division' to define 'sophist'. This raises questions about kinds of imitation and fake, then about the more general problem of negation, where in the course of a complex discussion the 'Eleatic stranger' criticizes views held by 'the Friends of the Forms' (probably Plato's own earlier doctrine). How can we say what is not? How are false judgements meaningful, how can there be false opinions, imitations, images, pictures, deceptions, copies, products of mimesis? These are the stock-in-trade of the sophist, who is at last defined as an ironical, ignorant, fantastical image-maker who attempts to escape censure by denying the existence of falsehood and the validity of reason. He runs away into the darkness of not-being and feels his way about by practice (254 a). The dialogue explains that if we are to see how false judgements are significant we must avoid the old Eleatic confrontations of absolute being with absolute not-being. (The stranger admits to being a bit of a parricide where Father Parmenides is concerned.) Theaetetus is led to agree that not-being does seem to be rather interwoven with being (240 c), and the stranger explains that not-being is not the opposite of being, but that part of being which is different or other (257-8). When we deny that something is X, we are not denying that it *is*, but asserting that it is other. This is possible because the world is neither a dense unity nor an inapprehensible flux, but an orderly network of same-nesses and differences (249). This network ($\sigma\upsilon\mu\pi\lambda o\kappa\acute{\eta}$) makes possible falsehood and deception, and also truth and language. What are thus systematically connected are the Forms, here figuring as classes. 'We derive significant speech from the inter-weaving of the Forms' (259 e). This interweaving depends upon the pervasive presence of certain 'great kinds', very general structural concepts or logical features: existence, same, different, rest, motion. These are compared to vowels which join other letters together in a limited number of permissible groupings (253 a). Reality is such that some things are compatible, others incompatible, some arrangements are possible, others impossible (253 c). (Wittgenstein, solving the same problem, offers similar arguments in the *Tractatus*. On the relation between *Theaetetus* and *Sophist*, with some mention of Wittgenstein, see McDowell's commentary on *Theaetetus* 201-2.) The question of the Forms is not just a question about one and many to be answered by a dialectic of classification, as mentioned at *Philebus* 16 and *Phaedrus* 266 b and *Laws* 965. It is a question of logical structure, meaning. This is the structure desiderated by Socrates at *Parmenides* 130 a. It is also glanced at (but without reference to Forms) in the *Theaetetus* (185-6) as part of the argument against regarding knowledge as

perception. In the *Republic* an interlocking network
(σύμπλοκη, 476 a) of Forms is rather obscurely indicated
(they have 'necessary relations' as in mathematics?), and the
liberated mind is pictured (511 c) as moving about among
them with no intermediary. ('I don't quite understand',
says Glaucon. The idea of Good as first principle is never
really explained.) In the *Phaedo* (99 e) Socrates admitted that
he could not look at the sun and had to turn to *logoi* (propositions, discourse), which he added were not to be thought
of as images. (That is, speech, not objects of perception.)

What the *Sophist* at last makes clear is that the Form
system is available to us only in discourse. Thinking is inner
speech, 263 e, 264 a, and *Theaetetus* 190 a. (Plato's argument
does not in fact depend on this identification which is rightly
denied by Wittgenstein, *Investigations*, p. 217. See also
Tractatus 4.002.) This is where truth and knowledge live,
and plausibility and falsehood too. Because reality is thus
systematic (because of the orderly intrusion of not-being
into being), writing and imitation and forgery and art and
sophistry are possible, and we are able meaningfully and
plausibly to say what is not the case: to fantasize, speculate,
tell lies, and write stories. In such a world the sophist, as
charlatan and liar, is a natural phenomenon, since for truth
to exist falsehood must be able to exist too. Moreover, if
knowledge lives at the level of discourse we cannot (as far
as the *Sophist* is concerned), in the ultimate perhaps mystical
(quasi-aesthetic) sense envisaged earlier, know the Forms.
The *Phaedo* speaks of an escape from the body and even the
Theaetetus (176 b) tells us to flee to the gods. The *Sophist*
discusses knowledge without insisting upon such removals.
The image of knowledge as direct acquaintance, as seeing
with the mind's eye (although Plato does use it again later)
here gives way to the conception of knowledge as use of
propositions and familiarity with structure. Truth lies in discourse not in visions; so neither the little individual particulars (whose unknowability the *Theaetetus* ended by
admitting) nor the Forms as separated supersensible

individuals, are directly accessible to the mind. The sophist is pictured at 254 a as being in the Cave. But the imagery of spiritual progress is absent, and the dialogue makes a less strong claim for knowledge than that rejected in the *Theaetetus* (that knowledge is perception) or put forward in the *Republic* (that it is, somehow, being face to face with the Forms).

It is now perhaps possible to see deeper reasons for Plato's hostility to writing and to the practice of imitation, including mimetic art. One is struck by the similarity of the venomous description of the sophist to the descriptions of the artist which are found elsewhere. If falsehood has to be possible then a whole art of deceiving can exist (264 d). The ideal of knowledge is to see face to face, not (*eikasia*) in a glass darkly. However, truth involves speech and thought is mental speech, so thought is already symbolism rather than perception: a necessary evil. (On the ambiguity of necessary evils, and the problems of the *Sophist* generally, see Jacques Derrida's brilliant essay *La Pharmacie de Platon*.) The best we can hope for is the flash of ultra-verbal understanding which may occur in live philosophical discussion when careful informed trained speech has set the scene. (*Seventh Letter* 341 c.) Language itself, spoken, is already bad enough. Writing and mimetic art are the introduction of further symbols and discursive *logoi* or quasi-*logoi* which wantonly make a poor situation even worse and lead the mind away in the wrong direction. (Derrida comments on Plato's frequent use of the word φάρμακον, drug, to mean what can kill or cure. Writing is described as a φάρμακον at *Phaedrus* 275 a.) The sophist is odious because he plays with a disability which is serious, glories in image-making without knowledge, and, living in a world of fictions, blurs the distinction between true and false (260 d). He is a subjectivist, a relativist, and a cynic. In the process of division which leads to the definition of the sophist, even the artist-copyist is allotted a slightly higher place in the realm of *eikasia*, the shadow world of the Cave. The sophist is described as an εἰρωνικὸς μιμητής, an ironical imitator. (εἰρωνικός is sometimes translated 'insincere', but 'ironical' best conveys the idea of cautious intelligent doubletalk which is required here.) Ironical, as opposed to naive, imitators have been disturbed by philosophy and (286 a) through experiences of the hurly-burly of argument uneasily suspect that they are really ignorant of what they publicly profess to understand. We may recall here the ἀδολεσχίας καὶ μετεωρολογίας φύσεως πέρι, the discussion and lofty speculation about the nature of things, mentioned in the *Phaedrus* (269 e), of which all great art stands in need, and which Pericles was so lucky to pick up a smattering of from Anaxagoras. We are also reminded of the description of the artist in Book X of the *Republic* (599 c) as a false plausible know-all who can 'imitate doctors' talk'. The artist begins indeed to look like a special sort of sophist; and not the least of his crimes is that he directs our attention to particulars which he presents as intuitively knowable, whereas concerning their knowability philosophy has grave and weighty doubts. Art undoes the work of philosophy by deliberately fusing knowledge by acquaintance and knowledge by description.

The argument so far has been about art, and it is time now to talk about beauty, to which Plato gives by contrast such an important role. Beauty as a spiritual agent, in Plato, excludes art. Plato's work is, as I said, largely concerned with ways to salvation. We may speak of a (democratic) 'way of justice' which, without necessarily leading to true enlightenment, is open to anyone who is able to harmonize the different levels of his soul moderately well under the general guidance of reason. The characteristic desires of each level would not be eliminated, but would in fact under rational leadership achieve their best general satisfaction. The baser part is really happier if rationally controlled. This reasonable egoism would be accessible to the lower orders in the *Republic*. Plato certainly thought that few could be 'saved', but allowed that many might lead a just life at their own spiritual level. (The doubts raised at the end of Book IX of the *Republic* concern surely the existence of the ideal state as a real state, and not any dubiety about its far more important efficacy as an allegory of the soul.) The *Laws* presents a somewhat grimmer picture of the status of the ordinary just man. Plato remarks that most people want power not virtue (687 c) and must be trained by pleasure and pain to prefer justice. (Art can help here.) Of course justice is in fact pleasanter as well as better than injustice, but even if it were not it would be expedient to say that it was (653, 663). Political systems make men good or bad. The way of justice is subservient to two higher ways, which I shall call 'the way of Eros', and 'the way of Cosmos'. In so far as justice involves a harmony of desires, and if all desires are (as Plato tells us at *Symposium*, 205 e) for the good in the guise of the beautiful, then the way of justice could lead into higher ways, and even the humblest citizen could suffer a divine disturbance. In the *Republic*, although 'the beautiful' is mentioned (for instance at 476 b), mathematical studies rather than science or love of beauty introduce us to the highest wisdom; and although mathematics too are 'beautiful' this is not yet emphasized.

In his conception of the beautiful Plato gives to sexual love and transformed sexual energy a central place in his philosophy. Sexual love (Aphrodite) as cosmic power had already appeared in Presocratic thought in the doctrines of Empedocles (fr. 17). Plato's Eros is a principle which connects the commonest human desire to the highest morality and to the pattern of divine creativity in the universe. Socrates more than once claims to be an expert on love (*Symposium* 177 e, 212 b; *Phaedrus* 257 a). In spite of Plato's repeated declaration that philosophers should stay chaste and his requirement that the soul must try to escape from the body, it is the whole Eros that concerns him, and not just some passionless distillation. The Eros described to Socrates by Diotima in the *Symposium* is not a god but a daemon, a mediating spirit of need and desire, the mixed-up child of Poverty and Plenty. He is poor and homeless, a sort of magician and sophist, always scheming after what is good and beautiful, neither wise nor foolish but a lover of wisdom. We desire what we lack. (Gods do not love wisdom since they possess it.) This Eros, who is lover not beloved, is the ambiguous spiritual mediator and moving spirit of mankind. Eros is the desire for good and joy which is active at all levels in the soul and through which we are able to turn toward reality. This is the fundamental force which can release the prisoners and draw them toward the higher satisfactions of light and freedom. It is also the force which finds expression in the unbridled appetites of the tyrant (who is described in Books VIII–IX of the *Republic*). There is a limited amount of soul-energy (*Republic* 458 d), so, for better or worse, one desire will weaken another. Eros is a form of the desire for immortality, for perpetual possession of the good, whatever we may take the good to be. No man errs willingly; only the good is always desired as genuine (*Republic* 505 d), and indeed only the good is desired. This desire takes the form of a yearning to create in and through beauty (τόκος ἐν καλῷ, *Symposium* 206 b), which may appear as sexual love (*Laws* 721 b) or love of fame (the poets have immortal children) or love of wisdom. (These are the three levels of desire explored in the *Republic*. Desire must be purified at all levels.) Diotima goes on to tell Socrates of these erotica into which even he may be initiated, although the true mysteries lie beyond. The initiate is not to rest content with beauty in one embodiment, but to be drawn onward from physical to moral beauty, to the beauty of laws and *mores* and to all science and learning and thus to escape 'the mean slavery of the particular case'. Carnal love teaches that what we want is always 'beyond', and it gives us an energy which can be transformed into creative virtue. When a man has thus directed his thoughts and desires toward beauty of the mind and spirit he will suddenly receive the vision, which comes by grace, θείᾳ μοίρᾳ, of the Form of Beauty itself, absolute and untainted and pure, αὐτὸ καθ᾽ αὑτὸ μεθ᾽ αὑτοῦ μονοειδὲς ἀεὶ ὄν. F. M. Cornford (*The Unwritten Philosophy*) excellently says 'the best commentary on the *Symposium* is to be found in the Divine Comedy'. He quotes the end of *Purgatorio* Canto XXVII. As Dante parts from the human wisdom of Virgil, and experiences the magnetic pull of divine wisdom in the person of Beatrice, he feels (like the soul in the *Phaedrus*) the growth of wings. Virgil tells him that happiness, which mortals seek in so many forms, will now at last let all his hunger rest, and henceforth his own perfected will and desire will be his rightful guide. *Tratto t'ho qui con ingegno e con arte: lo tuo piacere omai prendi per duce.*

The *Symposium* and the *Phaedrus* are two of the great erotic texts of literature. The *Phaedrus* describes spiritual love in the most bizarre and intense physical terms. (How the soul grows its wings, 251.) Plato is here too in softened mood toward poetry, since he allows that the good poet is a divinely inspired madman. However the highest form of divine madness is love of beauty, that is, falling in love (249 d). We love beauty because our soul remembers having seen it when before birth it saw the Forms unveiled: 'perfect and simple and happy visions which we saw in the pure light, being ourselves pure' (250 c). But when the soul becomes incarnate it partially forgets, and is but confusedly reminded when it sees the earthly copies of the Forms. The copies of wisdom, justice, temperance are usually obscure to the mind of the incarnate soul, but beauty in its instances is most clearly seen (ἐκφανέστατον), most moving, most reminiscent of the vision of it in heavenly purity. What a frenzy of love wisdom would arouse if it could be looked at with such clarity. Plato continues his exposition with the image of the soul as a charioteer with a good and a bad horse. As they approach the beloved the bad lustful horse rushes forward and has to be savagely restrained while the good horse is obedient and modest. Beauty shows itself to the best part of the soul as something to be desired yet respected, adored yet not possessed. Absolute beauty, as the soul now recalls it, is attended by chastity. Love prompts *anamnesis* and the good comes to us in the guise of the beautiful, as we are also told in the *Philebus*.

This account, half mythical, half metaphysical, graphically suggests both the beginning and the end of the awakening process. We restlessly seek various 'goods' which fail to satisfy. Virtue in general may not attract us, but beauty presents spiritual values in a more accessible and attractive form. The beautiful in nature (and we would wish to add in art) demands and rewards attention to something grasped as entirely external and indifferent to the greedy ego. We cannot acquire and assimilate the beautiful (as Kant too explains): it is in this instructive sense transcendent, and may provide our first and possibly our most persisting image (experience) of transcendence. 'Falling in love', a violent process which Plato more than once vividly describes (love is abnegation, abjection, slavery) is for many people the most extraordinary and most revealing experience of their lives, whereby the centre of significance is suddenly ripped out of the self, and the dreamy ego is shocked into awareness of an entirely separate reality. Love in this form may be a somewhat ambiguous instructor. Plato has admitted that Eros is a bit of a sophist. The desire of the sturdy ego (the bad horse) to dominate and possess the beloved, rather than to serve and adore him, may be overwhelmingly strong. We want to de-realize the other, devour and absorb him, subject him to the mechanism of our own fantasy. But a love which, still loving, comes to respect the beloved and (in Kantian language again) treat him as an end not as a means, may be the most enlightening love of all. Plato's insistence that (homosexual) love should be chaste may be read literally, but also as an image of the transcendent and indomitable nature of beauty. That chaste love teaches is indeed a way of putting the general moral point of the erotic dialogues. Plato commends orderly married love in the *Laws*, and announces equality of the sexes. But family life did not touch his imagination and he does not suggest that here essentially unselfishness is to be learnt: a fact which has earned him the hostility of some critics. The metaphysical contention which is so passionately enveloped in the erotic myths is to the effect that a sense of beauty diminishes greed and egoism and directs the energy of the soul in the direction of the real and the good. In so far as this contention is argued by Plato via the Theory of Forms (which he himself admits to be riddled with difficulties), it may appear obscure and less than convincing. What is more convincing and very much more clear (and to some extent separable from the full-dress metaphysical system) is the moral psychology which we are offered here and in the *Republic*: a psychology which implicitly provides a better explanation of evil (how good degenerates into egoism) than Plato's more strictly philosophical arguments have been able to give us elsewhere, for instance in the *Philebus*. Eros is the desire for good which is somehow the same even when a degenerate 'good' is sought.

The comparison with Freud is an interesting and an obvious one, and would suggest itself even without Freud's own clear announcement, made several times, of his debt to Plato, and also to Empedocles. 'The enlarged sexuality of psychoanalysis coincides with the Eros of the divine Plato' (*Three Essays on the Theory of Sexuality*, preface to the third edition). Freud certainly follows an important line in Plato's thought when he envisages sex as a sort of universal spiritual energy, an ambiguous force which may be destructive or can be used for good. Freud also makes a tripartite division of the soul and pictures the health of the soul as a harmony of the parts. Freud like Plato (*Republic* 439), and following Empedocles (Love and Strife), first divided the soul in two, picturing it as a horseman or a class-divided state. His reasons for preferring a trio are the same as Plato's: an unmediated fight does not present a realistic picture of human personality. Kant had his own clear reasons for refusing mediation. Hume's attempts to mediate produce some of his best work. Plato's psychology would have benefited from a more prolonged study of the central area. Plato often speaks of the soul as being sick and in need of therapy. Both Plato and Freud wish to heal by promoting awareness of reality. Only Freud holds that we grasp reality through the ego and not through the 'critical punishing agency' of the ideal; whereas Plato holds that, above a reasonable egoism, there is a pure moral faculty which discerns the real world and to which sovereignty properly belongs. To put it another way, Plato is in favour of religion and the Father: it would be hard to overestimate the effect upon him of the death of Socrates, and although he never 'invents' a full-dress Father-God, his work abounds in images of paternity; while Freud is against religion and against fathers. Freud bars the way to the top and gives the ego the right to supreme control. Of course Plato's Eros, the daemonic negotiator between God and man, represents a sexuality which is almost entirely (perhaps for incarnate beings never entirely) able to be transfigured. Since the real is the good our energy is 'originally' pure. Freud, on the other hand, sees sexual energy as (rather precariously) climbing from a natural to an ideal level. Both thinkers share the important idea of the soul (mind) as an organic totality, strongly internally related and with a limited available material. 'Anyone who knows anything of the mental life of human beings is aware that hardly anything is more difficult for them than to give up a pleasure they have once tasted. Really we never can relinquish anything, we only exchange one thing for something else. When we appear to give something up, all we really do is to adopt a substitute.' (*The Relation of the Creative Writer to Day-Dreaming, Collected Papers*, vol. iv.) Plato would agree. Never has a philosopher more clearly indicated that salvation concerns the whole soul: the soul must be saved entire by the redirection of its energy away from selfish fantasy toward reality. Plato does not imagine that dialectic can save us, and indeed it will not be possible, unless the whole soul, including its indestructible baser part, is in harmony. Plato is in this respect a relentless psychological realist and more than once describes the soul as governed by mechanical gravitational forces which make change for the better very difficult. In morose moments in the *Laws* Plato even speaks like a determinist (we are puppets dangling from strings of impulse, 732 e), but elsewhere (904 b) he makes the growth of character depend on our will and the general trend of our desires. The transmigration myth at *Phaedrus* 247 pictures the aspiring soul as subject to some kind of natural gravity, and so does the rather grim last judgement at the end of the *Republic*. How far Plato 'believed' these and other doctrines which he inherited from the Pythagoreans and used for his own purposes has been much debated. But whatever his dogma, there is little doubt about his psychology. Justice is in this respect automatic. It does not seem to me that Plato has softened the old 'justice of Zeus' (see Hugh Lloyd-Jones's interesting argument in his book of that name); he has made its operation more sophisticated and considerably more just. We cannot escape the causality of sin. We are told in the *Theaetetus* (176–7) that the inescapable penalty of wickedness is simply to be the sort of person that one is, and in the *Laws* (904 c,d) that evil-doers are in Hades in this world. Wittgenstein said of Freud that 'he was influenced by the nineteenth-century idea of dynamics' (*Conversations on Freud*). Perhaps he was; but the dynamic model is already in Plato. Nor can one doubt that the concept of *anamnesis* influenced Freud's idea of the timeless and inaccessible unconscious mind. When Freud was twenty-three he translated an article bearing on *anamnesis* by J. S. Mill (See Rieff, *Freud*, 1959, p. 364). However, I know of no explicit reference by him to the doctrine.

Plato's Eros inspires us through our sense of beauty, but Eros is a trickster and must be treated critically. We have been told in the *Laws* (687 b) that the human soul desires omnipotence. The energy which could save us may be employed to erect barriers between ourselves and reality so that we may remain comfortably in a self-directed dream world. Freud's condition of neurosis represents this refusal of reality in favour of magical self-deception. The neurotic 'mistakes an ideal connection for a real one' and 'over-estimates the psychic process as opposed to reality'. Let us here, still led by Freud, look back again from Eros to art. Freud says

in *Totem and Taboo*, 'only in art has the omnipotence of
thought been retained in our civilization'. He shares Plato's
deep mistrust of art, as well as his interest in the nature of
inspiration, only of course Freud, confronted with the grandeur of the European tradition at its most confident (it is
less confident now) does not dare to be too rude to art.
'Before the problem of the creative artist analysis must,
alas, lay down its arms' (*Dostoevsky and Parricide, Collected
Papers*, vol. v). However, Freud does not in fact leave art un-
harrassed. He offers us elsewhere (in the paper on *The
Relation of the Creative Writer to Day-Dreaming*) a striking
and far from flattering definition of the work of art. Everyone has personal fantasies which are concealed and would be
repulsive if uttered. 'The essential *ars poetica* lies in the
technique by which our feeling of repulsion is overcome. . . .
The writer softens the egotistical character of the day-dream
by changes and disguises, and he bribes us by the offer of a
purely formal, that is aesthetic, pleasure in the presentation
of his fantasies.' The aesthetic bribe is described by Freud
as a 'fore-pleasure' (*Vorlust*) similar to those which lead
onward to orgasm. (This concept is discussed at more length
in *Three Essays on the Theory of Sexuality* iii. I.) The work
of art is then a magical pseudo-object (or εἰκών) placed between the artist and his client whereby they can both, se-
parately, pursue their private fantasy lives unchecked. 'True
enjoyment of literature proceeds from the release of tensions
in our minds. Perhaps much that brings about this result
consists in the writer putting us into a position in which we
can enjoy our day-dreams without reproach or shame.'

Plato says in the *Republic* (606 a) that the artist makes
the best part of the soul 'relax its guard'. One of the subtle-
ties of Freud's definition is that it is indifferent to the
'formal value' of the art work, since what is really active and
really attractive is the concealed fantasy. As W. H. Auden
says, a remark which could have been made by Plato, 'no
artist . . . can prevent his work being used as magic, for that
is what all of us, highbrow and lowbrow alike, secretly want

art to be' ('Squares and Oblongs', *Poets at Work*). One could hardly wish for a more thorough characterization of art as belonging to the lower part of the soul and producing what are essentially shadows. (The art object as material thing, a piece of stone or paper etc., would be classed with ordinary visible sensa; what the artist and his client 'see' would be the shadow.) W. D. Ross says that 'Plato is no doubt in error in supposing that the purpose of art is to produce illusion.' In fact Plato's view of art as illusion is positive and complex. Images are valuable aids to thought; we study what is higher first 'in images'. But images must be kept within a fruitful hierarchy of spiritual endeavour. What the artist produces are 'wandering images'. In this context one might even accuse art of specializing in the degradation of good desires, since the trick of the aesthetic veil enables the good to descend. The art object is a false whole which owes its air of satisfying completeness to the licensing of a quite other process in the quasi-mechanical fantasy life of the client, and also of the artist, who, as Plato frequently pointed out, probably has little idea of what he is at. The formal properties of the art object are delusive. The relation of art to the unconscious is of course at the root of the trouble. Put in Platonic terms, art is a sort of dangerous caricature of *anamnesis*. The 'un-limited' irrational nature of pleasure makes it suspect, and art has a conspiracy with pleasure which is the more dama-ging since it is partly secret. As explained in the *Philebus* the pleasures of any art except the very simplest are impure. (This is likely to be true upon any reasonable definition of 'pure' and 'impure'.) As escapism, art is an expert in 'pleasure by contrast', which though doubtless welcome to wretched suffering mortals, compares poorly with (for instance) the pure and positive pleasures of learning. The highest pleasure lies in the contemplation of the changeless, where there is calm clear perception. The element of the 'unlimited' in art pleasure comes from its connection with the purely egoistic unconscious (in Freudian terms) and privily robs art of ἀλήθεια, truthfulness and realism. Art has no discipline which ensures veracity; truth in art is notoriously hard to estimate critically. Human beings are natural liars, and sophists and artists are the worst. Art undermines our sense of reality and encourages us to believe in the omnipotence of thought. Thus the supposed 'content' of art leaks away into the 'unlimited' and no genuine statement is made. Truth must be very sure of herself (as she is in mathematics) before she allows any connection with art: so, if there must be art, better to stick to embroidery and wallpaper.

Plato was not unaware of neurosis as mental disease, as distinct from moral depravity or the wilful ignorance for which ἔλεγχος, ruthless questioning, was the suitable purge. Although he usually took a rather tough view of the θερεπεία ψυχῆς, he says at *Timaeus* 86 b that folly is a disease of the soul, and at *Laws* 731 tells us to talk gently to remediable offenders; it is repeated in both contexts that no man errs willingly. The profound action of music upon the soul is of course often mentioned, and there is a reference in the *Laws* (790) to art as a cure for anxiety states. (On this see E. R. Dodds, *The Greeks and the Irrational*, Chapter III.) This is of course an aspect of the magical nature of art so often emphasized by Plato. Freud saw how art can stabilize neurosis without removing it. The artist comes to terms with his frailties (even with his vices) by using them in art, thus producing a stability which may be (from the point of view of mental health) less than satisfactory. The destructive power of the neurosis is foiled by art; the art object expresses the neurotic conflict and defuses it. This sort of (as it might be seen by Freud or Plato) 'imperfect' and misleading transformation or pseudo-cure would especially characterize the artist as 'ironical copyist' (as opposed to naive fantasist) who has been disturbed by argument and speculation: a little knowledge of philosophy or psychology. Such a 'cure' may be seen as arresting progress. (Freud of course did not envisage perfect cures, and would doubtless have regarded many artists as solving their problems quite inadequately.) There is an element here of *corruptio optimi pessima*. The poet is a menace because he can corrupt even the good man, and the more sophisticated the art the more potentially dangerous. To revert to the imagery of the Cave, we might think of the ironical artist as having moved out of the shadowy region of *eikasia* as far as the fire, which he takes as his sun. (The fire in the cave corresponds to the sun in the outside world, *Republic* 517 b.) Here he can recognize for what they are the objects which cast the shadows. The bright flickering light of the fire suggests the disturbed and semi-enlightened ego which is pleased and consoled by its discoveries, but still essentially self-absorbed, not realizing that the real world is still somewhere else. (The 'lower' general education offered in the *Republic* could promote a moderate and fairly rational egoism.) The Delphic precept does not enjoin that kind of self-knowledge. The true self-knower knows reality and sees, in the light of the sun, himself as part of the whole world. In spite of their different aims, it is arguable that Plato and Freud mistrust art for the same reason, because it caricatures their own therapeutic activity and could interfere with it. Art is pleasure-seeking self-satisfied pseudo-analysis and pseudo-enlightenment.

Beauty then is too important a matter to be left to artists, or for art to meddle with at all except at a controllably simple level of, for instance, mathematical pattern. Nature educates us, art does not. This means: not statues, but boys. (We learn reality through the pains of rationally controlled human love, *Symposium* 211 b.) It also means a proper attention to the physical world around about us. The nature which Plato here regards as so educational is not of course the nature of the Romantics (trees and fields have no message), nor is it Kant's Sublime. Even to say that the perishable aspect of the natural scene defeats possessive ends is to take up a later viewpoint. What interests Plato in nature is pattern, necessity which is the test of truth: what turns opinion into certainty. Study of form liberates the mind, but it must be hard non-pliable real form, not the complicit pliable disingenuous forms of art. Encounter with the necessary leads to knowledge of the eternal and changeless. This educational truthful 'hardness' of the real is seen by Plato at first most evidently in mathematics, which plays the crucial mediating role in the education system of the *Republic*. Mathematics leads us beyond the lower (softer) education (described in Book III) which consists of (carefully selected) stories, music, poetry, where an uncriticized imagery is the best available vehicle of such truth as can be grasped. Understanding of how mathematics is independent of sense experience leads us to understand how the Forms are; and necessary mathematical relations suggest necessary relations between Forms. The early Socrates of the *Apology* and the *Phaedo* rejected scientific studies, and at *Republic* 529–30 we are told to use the tapestry of the heavens to remind us of geometry, but not to imagine that the stars can be objects of knowledge. Later Plato finds this necessary 'hardness' in the 'logical' rigidity of the Form world (*Sophist*), and later still in certain intimations of cosmic reason (*Timaeus*), where the stars (47 a) now suggest number and time and also researches into the nature of the universe. In the *Laws* astronomy has become a respectable subject, since the divine intelligence is revealed in all things (966 a) and science will not necessarily lead to atheism. The Athenian regrets not having studied astronomy when he was young (821). The gods are not jealous of their secrets, but glad if we can become good through studying them (*Epinomis* 988 b). Already however in the *Republic*, and in the context of the attack on art, Plato has set the cosmic 'way' within the reach of the craftsman. Measuring and counting are 'felicitous aids' (602 d) by which reason leads the soul from appearance to reality. The paradoxes of sense experience inspire us to philosophy, and our respect for and satisfaction in necessary form, whether in mathematics or in nature, tend to fortify our rational faculties. (Philosophy since Plato has largely favoured just these starting-points.) The object which appears to bend as it enters water provokes a lively puzzlement about what is real, and 'that part of the soul which trusts measuring and calculating is the best' (*Republic* 602 c, 603 a). How our satisfaction in measurement and symmetry and harmony in the world about us is our sense of its reality and beauty has been explained in the *Philebus*; and the truth-loving Eros can inspire the carpenter as well as the mathematician. But art always wants to take over the natural scene, and indeed affects how we see it. The self-indulgent imagination of the artist and his client tend to smooth out the contradictions of the world of natural necessity. The painter is content with the 'bent' object and prepared to celebrate it as it is (and in literature *mutatis mutandis*). Art baffles the motive to probe. It fascinates and diverts the Eros which should, whether through love of people or of cosmic form, conduct us to philosophy. Art gives magically induced satisfaction to the lower part of the soul, and defaces beauty by mixing it with personal sorcery. Beauty gives us an immediate image of good desire, the desire for goodness and the desire for truth. We are attracted to the real in the guise of the beautiful and the response to this attraction brings joy. To overcome egoism in its protean forms of fantasy and illusion (*per tanti rami cercando*) is automatically to become more moral; to see the real is to see its independence and ergo its claims. The proper apprehension of beauty is joy in reality through the transfiguring of desire. Thus as we respond we experience the transcendence of the real and the personal ego fades as, in the words of the *Symposium* (210 d), we 'escape from the mean petty slavery of the particular case and turn toward the open sea of beauty'.

Plato's connection of the good with the real (the ambiguous multiform phenomenon of the ontological proof) is the centre of his thought and one of the most fruitful ideas in philosophy. It is an idea which at an instinctive level we may readily imagine that we understand. We do not have to believe in God to make sense of the motto of Oxford University, displayed upon an open book, *Dominus illuminatio mea*. And I shall argue later that, for all its sins, art can show us this connection too. But what is the 'reality' to which Eros moves us and from which art allegedly diverts us? The Theory of Forms was invented to explain this, and the *Parmenides* and the *Sophist* exhibited some of the resultant difficulties. The relation of Forms to particulars remains persistently problematic as Plato moves uncertainly from a metaphor of participation to one of imitation, and increasingly emphasizes that the Forms are 'separate'. The Forms are more like 'imminent universals' at the start, and 'transcendent models' later on. The theory is in evident process of transition in the *Parmenides*. The *Sophist* represents a moment of discovery and offers a new theory. What is of importance here is not the puzzling relation of Forms to particulars, but the now more comprehensible relation of Forms to each other. Because of what is possible and impossible in the Form world, reality has deep rigid structure and discourse is possible. Dialectic, becoming more specialized, can thenceforth operate more confidently though less ambitiously. The philosopher in the *Republic* returns to the Cave, and once he is used to it, can manage better than the captives (520 c). (He gives up studying and goes into politics, for which his studies have trained him.) Later on (*Theaetetus* 172–4, *Philebus* 58 c, *Seventh Letter* 344 e) the implication is that dialectic is 'for its own sake', and the philosopher is confused by practical life. The Form of the Good in the *Republic* is a first principle of explanation and also (if we follow the image of the sun), some sort of general first cause. The *Sophist* is concerned with the logical rather than the moral Forms, and although 'soul' makes its appearance as a principle of life and movement, this idea still lacks moral and theological development, and Plato's earlier 'psychology' still best explains the role of goodness. Art, of course, comes under this 'psychological' heading, together with the problem of appearance and reality as originally envisaged. It remains Plato's (surely correct) view that the bad (or mediocre) man is in a state of illusion, of which egoism is the most general name, though particular cases would of course suggest more detailed descriptions. Obsession, prejudice, envy, anxiety, ignorance, greed, neurosis, and so on and so on *veil* reality. The defeat of illusion requires moral effort. The instructed and morally purified mind sees reality clearly and indeed (in an important sense) provides us with the concept. The original role of the Forms was not to lead us to some attenuated elsewhere but to show us the real world. It is the dreamer in the Cave who is astray and elsewhere.

What here becomes of the problem of the relation of Forms to particulars, and is it still important? If dialectic is a kind of logic, together with a kind of classification involving a pursuit to *infimae species*, then the problem posed at the end of the *Theaetetus* about the unknowability of the particular may indeed remain, but may also be deemed trivial. In the early dialogues sense experience seems to be at least partly veridical in so far as particular things 'partake' of the Forms; and later on *Theaetetus* 155-7 offers a fairly straightforward (realistic) discussion of perception. In the *Republic*, where the Forms are transcendent, the objects of opinion diminish near the lower end of the scale from 'being' toward 'not-being' (478-9). The *Sophist* turns this awkward ontological distinction into a 'logical' one. But supposing what interests us is the reality which is penetrable to moral insight? (Logic can look after itself; ethics cannot.) What about mud, hair, and dirt (*Parmenides* 130 c), and in what sense if any are they to be 'given up'? The metaphor of knowledge as vision is not so easily eliminated, at either end of the scale of being. When the veil is removed and the rational and virtuous man sees reality, how much—indeed what—does he see? Are there things which somehow exist but which are irrelevant to serious thought, as Socrates was inclined to say in the *Parmenides*? Is it possible to *see* beyond the 'formal network'? (Instinct says yes.) What does the light of the sun reveal; and who sees the most minute particulars and cherishes them and points them out? As one batters here at the cage of language it is difficult to keep the artist out of the picture even when one is attempting to describe the good man. Of course we are in trouble here through doing what

Parmenides told Socrates he must do if he was really to be 'grabbed' by philosophy (*Parmenides* 130 d, e), that is let nothing go and see if what is true of one is true of all. From the point of view of the moralist it looks as if the argument which culminates in the *Sophist* has destroyed too much, since notably it has removed our direct vision of the Forms and their positive role as (somehow) sources of light and being. However Plato does not here abandon the problem of the reality and intelligibility of the sensible world, but begins to envisage it in a new way.

The early picture of the Forms is unsatisfactory not only because of the unclarified relation of these separate change-less perfect entities to a changing imperfect world, but also because the Forms are supposed to be the only realities. The transmigrating souls of the *Phaedo* and the *Phaedrus* are of unexplained and lesser dignity, although they 'resemble' the changeless (*Phaedo* 786); and in the *Phaedo* the sensible world appears as a fallen realm which is a gross irrelevant hindrance to true knowledge, philosophy, and virtue. Hence philosophers 'practise dying' (67 e). The earlier dialogues emphasize a contrast between what is moving and unreal and what is motionless and real. Vice is restless, so is art (*Republic* 605 a). The bad man and the artist see shifting shadows (εἴκονες), not a steady reality. The *Sophist,* however (248 e), exclaims with passion, 'Surely we shall not readily allow ourselves to be persuaded that motion and life and soul and intelligence are not really there in absolute being and that it neither lives nor thinks, but all solemn and holy and mindless is motionless and fixed.' Plato, led by the epistemological arguments of the *Parmenides* and the *Theaetetus*, is not ready fully to separate the psychological-moral idea that vice is a state of illusion from the problem of the reality and physical nature of the sensible cosmos. He has already, in Eros, established an authoritative active principle which can relate everything to the Forms. (The low Eros is the high Eros.) But Eros as mediator, and as 'redeemer', of the trivia of the ordinary world, is still a detached insight and a psychological myth.

The attribution of life and movement to ultimate being in the *Sophist* brings this 'mediation' into the area of philosophical argument; though inconclusively so since Plato soon returns again to 'explanation' by myth. To extend the possibility of knowledge (as opposed to opinion), he here conjures up a moving knower to follow a moving known, and gives a more definite status to the problem of the origin of motion. In doing so he creates a fundamental division in the structure of the ultimately real since κίνησις and ζωή and ψύχη and φρόνησις (movement, life, soul, intelligence) are now allowed somehow into the company of the still changeless Forms. This 'fissure', and the attempt to relate Forms to particulars by this method, raises its own insoluble problems, though it has also proved a great fountainhead of metaphysical imagery. Soul has already been described as the only self-mover and thus as the origin of motion at *Phaedrus* 245–6 and *Politicus* 272 b; and creative intelligence or mind (φρόνησις, νοῦς) now comes forward to be the supreme guide of soul, as life and movement are allowed to be intelligible. One result of this mediation is the extension of the power of Good into the details of the sensible world through a technique of active creation. Throughout his work Plato uses the imagery of *mimesis*, which the Theory of Forms necessitates but cannot explain. In a magnificent myth he at last frankly embraces the image and sanctifies the artist, while giving to the Forms a final radiant though mysterious role. There is only one true artist, God, and only one true work of art, the Cosmos.

In Raphael's divine vision of the School of Athens, Plato, holding the *Timaeus*, points with a single finger upward, while Aristotle, holding the *Ethics*, stretches out his extended hand toward the world. The *Timaeus* is an account of the creation of the world by God, wherein Christian thinkers from Origen to Simone Weil have had no difficulty in discerning the doctrine of the Trinity, and other thinkers 'with a little good will' (Paul Shorey) have been able to see quite a lot of modern physics. The rational and good Demiurge creates the cosmos and endows it with a discerning Soul. He works as well as he can, gazing at a perfect model (the Forms), to create a changing sensible copy of an unchanging intelligible original. He cannot, however, create perfectly because he is using pre-existent material which contains irrational elements, the 'wandering causes', which represent irreducible qualities tending toward some minimal non-rational order of their own. The activity of these causes is called 'necessity' (ἀνάγκη), meaning not mechanical system but a semi-random interruption of rational purposes. (See Cornford's commentary on 47–8. The Greeks were familiar with tools, not with machines.) The purposeful Demiurge is not omnipotent and cannot subdue the wandering causes, but *persuades* them, so as to create the best possible world. In this process the Forms remain entirely separate and untouched as they have always been. Their copied reflections appear ephemerally in the medium of space which is eternal and uncreated. (There is no Form of space, though there is a Form of time.) The Demiurge creates junior gods and human souls, and delegates to the gods the task of creating us. He is also a just judge, allotting destinies according to conduct. We, who belong both to being and to becoming, find our moral guidance in the cosmos itself, the work of the divine hand. The Demiurge creates the world because, being good and without envy, he wishes all things to be as like himself as possible, and he desires for human creatures that they shall achieve the best possible life.

Socrates said in the *Phaedo* (97–9) that he gave up reading Anaxagoras because no account was given of purposeful causation. The *Timaeus*, deliberately taking issue with Plato's evolutionary 'materialist' predecessors, offers a carefully modified quasi-teleological cosmogony in the form of a myth, wherein moral imagery and scientific speculation are remarkably blended. The Demiurge (Plato's portrait of the artist and a most attractive figure) is a new conception, palely foreshadowed in the *Philebus*. Plato's predecessors ('the wise' mentioned at *Gorgias* 508 a) had of course already

pictured the universe as 'order' (*Kosmos*); and Greek
theology had been tending gradually toward the separation of
a morally good sovereign Zeus from the other Olympian
gods. Plato's God is not, however, to be identified with this
new Zeus. Plato regarded the Olympians with a detached but
not totally irreverent scepticism. (See *Timaeus* 40 a, also
Cratylus 400 d, *Phaedrus* 246 c, *Epinomis* 984 d.) Nor is he at
all like the cosmic 'gods' of the Presocratics. And although
Plato quotes Pherecydes saying that Zeus became Eros to
create the world, the Demiurge is not Plato's Eros, though he
is related to him. The Demiurge looks towards the Forms
with rational passion and with a yearning to create (τόκος
ἐν κάλῳ), but he is a free divine being, not a needy daemon.
He is morally perfect (though not omnipotent) and lacks the
envious spite (φθόνος) which the Olympians so often felt
toward mortals. (The Greeks always feared this spite and
constantly expressed the fear in their literature.) On the
other hand he is unlike Jehovah and the Christian God in
that he does not require, or receive, worship or gratitude.
He wishes us well and hopes for our salvation (he admonishes
human souls at 42 d), but we are not necessarily at the centre
of his concern. He is probably more interested in the stars.
As *Laws* 903 c tells us, the cosmos does not exist for our
sake, we are not its end. And the message of the *Timaeus*, as
indeed of other dialogues including the *Republic*, is that we
exist, and must seek such perfection as may be available to
us, as parts of a whole.

The World Soul, developed from ideas in the *Sophist*,
completes Plato's Trinity. This mysterious Soul is an incarnation of spirit which pervades the whole sensible cosmos and
is created for this purpose by the Demiurge. At 44 a–b it is
hinted that the World Soul may not be entirely rational, and
it is certainly the most junior and least authoritative of the
trio, its two partners being uncreated. In terms of the (not
unrelated) Christian trinity the artist figure, the creative
Demiurge, occupies of course the position of the Holy Ghost,
not of God the Father. The Demiurge is active νοῦς, best

translated here as 'mind'. Absolute original authority rests
in the Forms, and the World Soul, incarnate spirit in the
realm of sense, is, it is implied, somewhat 'fallen' thereby (as
the incarnate Forms are 'fallen' in the *Phaedo*). If one may
here respond simply and naively to something so complex, I
confess that I find Plato's Trinity more morally radiant than
that of the Church. The theology of the *Timaeus* is also more
splendid than Plato's own further theological speculations in
Laws X. To suggest that God is not omnipotent has always
been a prime Christian heresy. The image of a morally perfect
but not all-powerful Goodness seems to me better to express
some ultimate (inexpressible) truth about our condition. The
Jehovah of *Genesis* is totally unlike the artist, human or
divine, in that he creates out of nothing and expects perfection. (Perhaps the Demiurge more intelligently realized
his limitations at the start, whereas Jehovah realized his
later and was correspondingly bad-tempered?) Also, the eternal
separate inviolate Forms seem to me a more profound image
of moral and spiritual reality than the picture of a personal
Father, however good. The forms represent the absolute and
gratuitous nature of the moral demand, so splendidly though
so differently emphasized by Kant, who also separated God
from our knowledge of moral perfection. The mythical Demiurge creates because active mind must move (that movement
belongs to ultimate being was recognized in the *Sophist*), and
he is moved by love for the Forms to attempt to imitate
them in another medium. Like the mortal artist he fails, both
because the other medium cannot (as he is well aware) re-
produce the original, and because the material resists his
conceptions and his powers. The result is a quite different
entity, which is the 'best possible'. The Platonic Trinity is a
development, and sub-division, of the concept of Eros. It
relates Eros to Cosmos, and expresses in an alternative and
more complex way the idea that Good attracts, an ingredient
of the ontological proof. A live force moves through the
created world towards Good. The Demiurge is here the
mediating figure between Being and Becoming. Good is seen

as beautiful in the purified or even semi-purified gaze of active mind. We are kin to νοῦς and no one errs willingly. In the Christian Trinity love passes continually between the three persons all of whom are in motion. In Plato's Trinity two partners are busy while one is still. The Demiurge is intelligently busy (and as independent causes proliferate his work must go on), while the World Soul is not quite sure what it is at, but does the best it can. Incarnate spirit, even in saints and geniuses, is muddled and puny. The Forms remain changeless and eternal. I am sure that one should resist the Christianizing view that the Forms yearn for realization or tend towards it. Such 'yearning' belongs entirely to the mythical Demiurge. Good is 'beyond being' as Plato says at *Republic* 509 b, and never really explains the idea. The question of course remains and must remain, why does the sensible world exist at all? Creation myths are not philosophical explanations. Plato never thought that they were, and he never philosophically clarified the relation between Forms and sensa.

The *Philebus* spoke of the difficulty of locating Good, and of how Good took refuge in the character of the Beautiful. The *Timaeus* exhibits this creative movement of Good into Beauty, as it also establishes as first cause Mind that looks to Good, and not Good itself. The Demiurge is in a state of activity while the Forms are in a state of rest. Beauty comes about through the persuasion of necessity by divine intelligence; everything that exists has both a necessary and a divine cause. Beauty belongs to God and must be sought only in him, as he makes it visible through the cosmos. The cosmos is in the highest and exemplary sense an aesthetic object, and indeed the only one. The Demiurge's satisfactions and his relation to his material are those of an artist. The material resists organization not as a scientist's material resists, when systems cannot yet be discerned, but as an artist's material resists, because it is in part fundamentally a jumble of which nothing can be made. (Possibly modern physics feels itself closer to the situation of the artist.) Of course the

Demiurge is a mythical being (to describe God is impossible, 28 c), but his partial defeat represents the failure of an earlier requirement: the availability to intelligence of perfect knowledge such as that envisaged in the *Republic*. There, what could be known could be known perfectly, and what could not be known was in danger of being deemed unreal and therefore nothing: a problem which was met in the *Sophist* by an explanation of God's logical limitations. Here, in the *Timaeus*, we see his corresponding difficulties as an applied physicist.

Plato, who at first rejected natural science, had by this time learnt a good deal more about it and cannot resist some scientific speculation, although he still distinguishes as strictly as ever between knowledge of being and opinion about becoming, and admits the latter with a smiling apology. We may 'for amusement' lay aside 'arguments about reality' and consider 'probable accounts of becoming' (59 c). This apology introduces some detailed and admittedly 'probable' explanations of natural phenomena. The more general and large-scale proceedings of the Demiurge are offered to us more confidently, together with clear indications of the limited scope of his power. The raw stuff of creation has inherent causal tendencies and the medium of space in which it is worked is also not made by the Demiurge, and though eternally real is not in fact entirely intelligible (52 b), but apprehended by a 'bastard reasoning' which leads us to 'dream' that 'everything is somewhere'. (A foreshadowing of Kant's problem: we experience space without understanding it.) Space is the reality which carries the transient flux and lends some being to even the most shadowy of appearances; though how this happens is admitted at 52 c to be somewhat astonishing and hard to describe. The Demiurge understands time since he creates it as a 'moving image of eternity' (time is circular), but it is not entirely clear that he understands space. A creative Soul is present in the *Laws*, again named as first cause (899 c), and we are told that *physis* is brought about by *techne* and *nous* (892 a–b), but these problems, which are grasped in the *Timaeus* in a great *élan* of sometimes half-playful artistry, are brought to no conclusion.

The interest of the dialogue is of course fundamentally moral, and the scientific conjectures never stray too far from a moral concern. Plato is not here discussing (and indeed never really discusses again) his persistent problem about the definition of knowledge and its limitations. The implication of the myth is that our claims must ever be modest ones, but this does not make the vision less inspiring. The *Timaeus* declares the intelligible reality of the whole material universe, not hitherto clearly asserted by Plato. His descriptions of it relate to our ordinary experience as do the descriptions offered by the modern physicist, and are not totally unlike these. The privilege of knowing by direct perception is transferred to the Demiurge, who can see both ends of the scale of being, the great uncreated Particulars and the little created ones. Through this image Plato is able, in a masterpiece of art which is radiant with joy, to 'solve' some of his old problems by relating creative Eros directly to the eternal authority of Good, and through it to the world. It is hard for the moralist to abandon the idea of this connection as something potentially direct, however difficult it may be to explain how we can 'know' anything of the sort. Art and the artist may indicate what lies just beyond the explanations offered by 'plain words', once the words have carefully made a place for revelation. And although 'officially' we humans may not be able to see into these mysteries, one mortal artist at least is self-contradictorily telling us about them.

In the context of his great mythical reconciliation, Plato assumes rather than demonstrates the Forms. An argument for their existence is given in the most curtailed but essential version at 51 d–e, where we are also told that only gods and very few men can possess knowledge. No other arguments, as such, are offered, but the position allotted to the Forms is in many ways more intelligible, at this point where perhaps Plato realizes the insolubility of the problems which they pose, than that which they occupied in the *Republic*, where Good was supposed to play a creative role (509 b). This role is taken over by the Demiurge who makes the cosmos as we experience it (including mud, hair, and dirt) upon an intelligible model, joining in every instance his divine causation to the necessary causation of the original stuff, and thereby sanctifying the cosmos and rendering it potentially penetrable to human reason. Beauty can then be discerned everywhere, though this is not emphasized by either Plato or the Demiurge whose interests tend to be rather grandiose. So it turns out that the artist copies the Forms after all, but he has to be God and even then cannot succeed perfectly. The separateness of the Forms is stated in the most uncompromising terms at 52 a. Their authority is absolutely unimpaired by the presence of the Demiurge; and in the mysterious magnificence of this assertion lies part of the deep sense of the whole theory.

This splendidly complex mythical image of the creative process suggests and indeed demands interesting analogies with art of the mortal variety, and these will be considered later. The Demiurge presents himself of course not only as an engineer with a knowledge of physics and chemistry, but as a geometer, architect, and as a musician (37 c). Vision is the most uplifting of human senses (47 b), but the fine art preferred by God is music, inaudible of course. (All art aspires to this condition?) The audible kind is allowed (47 c) to be of benefit to us. The construction of the human body interests the Demiurge, but he delegates the process of incarnation, together with the invention of a workable incarnate psyche, to his young subordinates, who are described (69 d) as infusing in generous quantities the 'dreadful and necessary' emotions required for human survival. (It sounds as if this is rather a perfunctory job.) In spite of some interesting and sympathetic remarks about psychosomatic disorders (89–90), Plato does not here concern himself much with our moral psychology: which does not mean that he has abandoned his earlier views on the subject. In the *Timaeus* he is looking at the situation from God's point of view, where evil appears as a failure to impose rational order. It must however be admitted that the later dialogues are less sanguine about human perfectibility. (Most orderings of the dialogues put *Phaedrus* before *Sophist*, *Sophist* before *Timaeus*, and *Laws* last.) The human species is perhaps (on any view) not the most successful or edifying ingredient of the cosmic art object.

Our best task (68-9) is to distinguish in created things between the divine and the necessary cause and seek to understand and conform ourselves to the divine cause, and to seek the necessary cause for the sake of the divine, since we cannot see the divine without the necessary; and thus to gain whatever happiness and holiness our nature admits of. In doing this we see the beauty of the world through studying the structural work of the divine architect, including his geometry and his logic. Our position, both as created beings and as, in our little way, creators, is however a humble one. The Creator who gazes at the eternal and intelligible produces what is good, but he who without intelligence simply copies the world of becoming produces something worthless (28 a). An intelligent use should be made of the arts (τέχναι), not to give irrational pleasure but to reduce disharmony, and for this purpose speech and music exist (47 c-d). The *Timaeus* takes a modest view of human insight and creative ability. The proper activity of the human artist is in simple ways to discern and emphasize and extend the harmonious rhythms of divine creation: to produce good design rather than pretentious rival objects. (Consider much Islamic art.) Such artists should, like other craftsmen, meticulously study the world so as to distinguish its appearance from its reality. Our relation to the divine pattern thus discerned must not be ambitiously mimetic (mimesis apes appearance), but rather participatory and continuous. The decent artist patiently sorts order out of disorder. To put it (as Plato does not) in terms with a Kantian ring: a good man does not copy another good man, playing him as an actor plays a role, but attempts to become himself a part or function of the divine intelligence. We were never told to 'copy' the Forms by producing something else, but only to become able to see them and thus in a sense to become like them. In the *Timaeus* myth they are more remote from us, seen by God and by him creatively transformed into another medium. Our humbler task, as part of creation, is to understand the Forms through the cosmic intelligence which is akin to our own. The artist must surrender his personal will to the rhythm of divine thought, as in the oriental doctrine of the Tao. If he practises mimetic art he may be guilty of a kind of blasphemy, as has always been recognized in Islam and in Judaism. The second commandment: Thou shalt not make unto thee any graven image, or any likeness of any thing that is in heaven above, or that is in the earth beneath, or that is in the water under the earth (Exodus 20:4). Of this Kant says, 'There is no more sublime passage in the Jewish law' (*Critique of Judgement* ii.274). There must be no picturesque mediator, no cue for egoistic drama. In the *Grundlegung* Kant firmly sets aside even Christ as mediator. Our sovereign and accessible guide is reason, and God is a remote object of faith. In the *Phaedo* Socrates fears that the sun will blind him, but in the *Republic* (516 b) the perfectly just man looks at the sun and 'is able to see what it is, not by reflections in water or by fantasms of it in some alien abode, but in and by itself in its own place'. This is the direct perception which the *Theaetetus* rejects as a possible description of knowledge. The God of the *Phaedrus* condemns writing because it interposes a speechless medium between the knower and the known. However, in the *Parmenides* the Forms as objects of knowledge are in trouble, and in the *Sophist* knowledge appears as familiarity with interwoven structure rather than acquaintance with individual realities. In the *Philebus* and the *Timaeus* Plato develops the idea, present mythically in the *Symposium* and the Phaedrus, of beauty as the mediator between us and Good; and is then the more meticulously anxious to keep this precious instrument away from the tarnishing hands of art.

Throughout his work Plato understands intellectual activity as something spiritual, the *love* of learning spoken of in the *Symposium* and the *Philebus*. Mediation through the beautiful takes place not only in intellectual studies but also through personal love and through the various *technai*, all kinds of craft and skill (excluding mimetic art) to which Plato at different times attaches importance. Love of beauty and desire to create inspire us to activities which increase our grasp of the real, and because they diminish our fantasy-ridden egoism are self-evidently good. Any *techne* gives us knowledge of reality through experience of necessity, and love of people does this too. Plato does not analyse in detail how selfish love changes into unselfish love, but the asides in the early dialogues do not suggest that this should simply be thought of as a transference of affection to philosophy. The wise lover does not only love the glamorous, but discerns the spiritual beauty of the unglamorous, a process movingly described by Alcibiades in his homage to Socrates at *Symposium* 215. Plato is more concerned in his later work, and indeed in the *Republic*, to show how the great structural features of the world, the subject-matter of logic and mathematics and (as he later sees it) of science, are beautiful and spiritually attractive. It is the attraction of beauty (good as harmony and proportion) which leads us into studies of the *a priori* and (to use a subsequent terminology) the synthetic *a priori*: pure studies yielding pure pleasures. In the mythology of the *Timaeus*, only passionate selfless unenvious mind can understand the world since passionate selfless unenvious mind made it, and we see in the light of the good, to return to the image of the sun. The cosmogony of the *Timaeus* is 'teleological' in that the Demiurge works purposively, but in doing so he seems to satisfy Kant's definition in that his purposiveness is without ulterior purpose. Order is obviously more beautiful and good than disorder, and the 'self-expression' of the Demiurge, who is generous and without envious φθόνος, takes place under the authority of an independent Model. Our participation in these joys must, however, be seen as modest. The contact with changeless truth brought about through insight into pure living mind can only for incarnate beings be limited and occasional, and we are likely to see more of necessary causes than of divine causes. The truth which we can grasp is something quiet, small in extent (*Philebus* 52 c), and to be found only in the lived real moment of direct apprehension out of which the indirectness of mimetic art and writing and perhaps language and discursive thought itself always tends to remove us. Those who want to be saved should look at the stars and talk philosophy, not write or go to the theatre.

How far Plato's own religious experience and practice remained separate from his philosophy and (as he more than once hints) ineffable, we are never likely to know. At *Phaedo* 69 d the 'enlightened ones' (βάκχοι) are identified with the true philosophers. It is a fair guess that his attitudes, as distinct from his arguments, owe much to 'the mysteries', and from this source he drew a condifence in divine providence and divine justice which he then expressed in philosophical and mythical form. (See Solmsen, *Plato's Theology*, chapter VII.) In some ways his 'pessimism' seems to increase as his theology is more consciously formulated. He never thought that we were μέγα τι, anything much, and the created beings of the *Timaeus* appear as small and helpless (seen of course by God), activated by 'necessary passions', and foreshadowing the 'puppets' of the *Laws*. The persuasion of the necessary by the divine is indeed not something into which we can see very far. Even to think of this as a Kantian 'idea of reason' is to view it in too rosy a light. Plato, for all his 'rationalism', never established reason as Kant does. Kant says that we gain enlightenment from the shock of reason's defeat by promptly feeling the strength and superior value of the 'defeated'. Plato does not console us with any readily available human reason (even incarnate reason in the form of the World Soul has its limitations), and as his thought develops the spiritual world gradually recedes. In the *Republic* we meet the spiritual in the guise of the necessary when paradoxes of sense experience disturb thoughtless acceptance and lead the mind to seek for tests of truth; and we are encouraged by the encounter with changeless knowable entities in mathematics. We are no better off in the *Timaeus* where active cosmic νοῦς has taken the place of the non-hypothetical first principle of the *Republic*. Indeed, though it must be kept in mind that the *Timaeus* is a theocentric myth, we seem to be worse off, in that there is no intelligible ladder of ascent, such as we have in the *Republic*, and the unimpeded vision of Good is reserved for the Demiurge. By the time the cosmic God arrives we seem to be further away from him than from the Zeus of the *Phaedrus* to whom Plato, in such lyrical and happy mood, declares his allegiance.

Plato allowed the image of a perfect unmixed good, which was the sole true object of desire, to summon up the (mythological) idea of a perfect creator-ruler. He never identified this 'God' with the Form of the Good. What the intellect seeks as perfect is, in thought at any rate, to be kept separate from the concept of God. The metaphor of moral vision, so important in the *Republic*, is maintained, but now while God sees the Forms, we see the stars (47 b). The cosmic deity seems more to express the inaccessibility of the absolutely real than its accessibility. In the early dialogues the spiritual world is so close that we seem to be God's children. In the *Timaeus* we are his grandchildren. In the *Laws* we are his toys. Our frailty is insisted upon. We are scarcely real (like, 889 c, the products of art), we are abject creatures, ταπεινοί, dangling from strings of pleasure and pain (*Laws* 644, 716, 902-7). In the *Phaedo* and the *Theaetetus* Plato uses images of escape to God. In the *Laws* the imagery is often of almost total separation and slavery. Plato's remarks about slaves (777) are (perhaps) surprisingly harsh, (perhaps) emotionally charged. Slaves should be addressed only with orders. (Vlastos comments on Plato's use of δουλεία for other forms of submission: *Slavery in Classical Antiquity*, ed. Finley.) The earlier part of the dialogue contains some scanty discussions of religious observance and popular cult, the more pictorial forms of religion suitable for those who can see the truth only 'in images'; and of course the rulers in the *Laws* are to use the charms of religion and art in the service of social stability, as the Egyptians did with such remarkable success (657, 799). Plato's own 'negative theology' appears as it were accidentally in grim asides which, like many important things in his work, often appear as jokes. Only God is a serious matter. We should not see our lives as serious toil for the sake of unserious play. For us, only play is 'serious' since we are playthings of the gods. Thus art (music) is valuable as an aid to divine grace (803). (These are deep words about the nature of play, religion, and art.) 'Everything is full of gods' (899 b); yet also God seems to have receded to an astronomical distance.

One of Plato's evident aims, both here and in the *Republic*, is the moral reform of religious concept and religious practice. Traditional city state religion was now undergoing a crisis of 'demythologization' not totally unlike that of present-day Christianity. So the *Laws* is not 'wantonly' exploring the possibility of new religious ideas. That such radical change was under general consideration we can see from the dramatists. Book X of the dialogue is devoted to more positive and theoretically coherent theological speculation, mythical in style though picking up a number of familiar philosophical themes. The cosmos again appears, and even more evidently so than in the *Timaeus*, as a harmoniously organized work of art wherein the parts are subservient to the total design. The supreme figures of the *Timaeus* appear here in altered guise, with the function of Soul much increased, and the Forms in eclipse. The many and the One receive mention at 965, in connection with the unity of virtue; and 895 d shows that Plato was still reflecting upon problems raised by the Forms, though we are not given the fruit of the reflection. Soul is now the cause of all things, including the details of sensible qualities, and is active everywhere. But although what it brings about resembles an art object, Soul is not, like the Demiurge, an

artist-copyist, and our world is at last real and not a copy.
There is, moreover, bad Soul as well as good Soul. This
dualism is not new in Plato's thought (*Republic* 397 b,
Politicus 270 a), though it is nowhere discussed at length.
Soul is still properly subject to the authority of Mind, but
may join itself with unreason (897 b). The best 'prelude' to
the laws (887 c) is refutation of atheism, and especially of
the view that the gods do not care. Being their 'property', we
are carefully and justly and indeed lovingly looked after.
Chattels are not necessarily despised, and the image is a pious
one, mentioned as a 'mystery' at *Phaedo* 62 b. Divine providence is just and good, even though evil men may prosper.
(Plato often muses upon the success of evil.) The gods care
for even the smallest things, but they do so also with a view
to the whole: just as a doctor looks at the part in relation to
the whole body, and statesmen look to the whole state and
craftsmen to the whole object (902). Individual souls matter,
and, as essential parts of the cosmic art object, move to their
appropriate places under the guidance of the divine gamester
(πεττευτής, 903 d). (God is not only always doing geometry,
he is always playing draughts.)

The intermittent, not uninvigorating gloom of the *Laws*
need not be construed as the cynicism of an ageing man,
though it is true that Plato's political adventures had mis-
carried and the great philosophical game of patience had
failed to come out. In fact the dialogue is not a tale of
gloomy repression, even if Plato's last State is in many ways
one which we would detest. The authoritarianism of the
Laws has been more publicized, especially of late, than has
its humane moral and political wisdom. (Modern criticism of
Plato as 'reactionary' is too often historically naive.) Plato
does not here attempt the major philosophical problems to
which he constantly returns in other dialogues, but his extremely minute discussions often illuminate his earlier more
generally stated theories. The practical detail is remarkable,
the advice often good, whether the talk is of property, law
and justice, or of exercises for pregnant women and the

importance of tidy hair and shoes. The life of moderation, of physical fitness and rational virtue, so often lauded earlier, is here exemplified in detail, and in this picture we may see how it is that the just are happier than the unjust. Art, within the limits of censorship, is treated with interest and even with a sort of fresh respect. Music and dance are described in animated detail, and *techné* is said (921 b) to be 'naturally clear and truthful'. The plain clear sustained relaxed eloquence of the moralizing is new and impressive, where here at last Plato speaks to us of morality without worrying about background theory, but taking it for granted and illustrating it out of his wide experience of states and peoples. We all suffer from self-love, so we must be gentle with remediable criminals and try to see how, in their case too, there was a sense in which they did not err willingly (731). Apparent 'equality' means real inequality if men do not receive what is appropriate; however, a more meticulous justice must always be tempered by tolerance and common sense (757). The *Laws* also contains (805) not only the earliest but probably the most uncompromising declaration ever made by a major philosopher of the equality of the sexes. Women can even do philosophy.

Plato, who treated the Olympians with such careful detachment, was of course well aware of the ambiguous nature of a busy personified 'God' or gods except as either necessary cult, or explanatory myth in a philosophical context. He always feared magic and almost the whole of his philosophy is a running fight against misleading and uncriticized images, some of them his own. Any seriously envisaged 'God', once liberated from Zeus, has to recede, since anything said about him is likely to mislead us. 'To find out the maker and father of all things is indeed a task, and having found him to explain him to all men is an impossibility' (*Timaeus* 28 c). In the *Laws* God appears as a theological device, as quasi-philosophical quasi-mythical theological speculation, or as an absence prompting bitter jokes. Escape from the Cave and approach to the Good is a progressive discarding of relative false goods, of hypotheses, images, and shadows, eventually seen as such. However, even the most enlightened discourse involves language, and dealing with the world is, as Plato usually envisages it, dealing with instances or copies of the Forms whose relation to their great originals can never be satisfactorily pictured. The glory of the Demiurge never dims that of the Form of the Good as it appears in splendour in the *Republic*. As difficulties emerged Plato changed his imagery, sometimes and finally abandoning philosophical argument altogether. He was always conscious of the possibility of being misunderstood, and the writer of the *Seventh Letter* expresses this anxiety with vehemence. St. John of the Cross says that God is the abyss of faith into which we fall when we have discarded all images of him. This is the point at which Plato starts making jokes.

We are now in a position to see the fundamentally religious nature of Plato's objections to art, and why he so firmly relegated it to the mental level of *eikasia*. Art is dangerous chiefly because it apes the spiritual and subtly disguises and trivializes it. Artists play irresponsibly with religious imagery which, if it must exist, should be critically controlled by the internal, or external, authority of reason. Artists obscure the enlightening power of thought and skill by aiming at plausibility rather than truth. Art delights in unsavoury trivia and in the endless proliferation of senseless images (television). Art is playful in a sinister sense, full of ($\phi\theta\acute{o}\nu o\varsigma$) a spiteful amused acceptance of evil, and through buffoonery and mockery weakens moral discrimination. The artist cannot represent or celebrate the good, but only what is daemonic and fantastic and extreme; whereas truth is quiet and sober and confined. Art is sophistry, at best an ironic *mimesis* whose fake 'truthfulness' is a subtle enemy of virtue. Indirectness and irony prevent the immediate relationship with truth which occurs in live discourse; art is thus the enemy of dialectic. Writing and painting introduce an extra distancing notation and by charm fix it in place. They create a barrier of imagery which arrests the mind, rigidifies the subject-matter, and is defenceless against low clients. The

true *logos* falls silent in the presence of the highest (ineffable)
truth, but the art object cherishes its volubility, it cherishes
itself not the truth, and wishes to be indestructible and
eternal. Art makes us content with appearances, and by
playing magically with particular images it steals the educational wonder of the world away from philosophy and
confuses our sense of direction toward reality and our
motives for discerning it. Through an unpurified charm
masquerading as beauty, art is 'most clearly seen'. 'Form'
thus becomes the enemy of knowledge. (See the end of
Death in Venice.) Art localizes the intelligence which should
be bent upon righting the proportions of the whole of life.
Form in art is for illusion and hides the true cosmic beauty
and the hard real forms of necessity and causality, and blurs
with fantasy the thought-provoking paradox. Art objects
are not real unities but pseudo-objects completed by the
fantasizing mind in its escape from reality. The pull of the
transcendent as reality and good is confused and mimicked.
The true sense of reality as a feeling of joy is deceitfully
imitated by the 'charm-joy' of art. There is very little good
art, and even that (*corruptio optimi pessima*) is dangerous.
Enjoyment of art deludes even the decent man by giving him
a false self-knowledge based on a healthy egoism: the fire in
the cave, which is mistaken for the sun, and where one may
comfortably linger, imagining oneself to be enlightened. Art
thus prevents the salvation of the whole man by offering a
pseudo-spirituality and a plausible imitation of direct intuitive knowledge (vision, presence), a defeat of the discursive
intelligence at the bottom of the scale of being, not at the
top. Art is a false presence and a false present. As a pseudo-
spiritual activity, it can still attract when coarser goals are
seen as worthless. We seek eternal possession of the good,
but art offers a spurious worthless immortality. It thus confuses the spiritual pilgrimage and obscures the nature of true
catharsis (purification). Its pleasures are impure and indefinite and secretly in league with egoism. The artist deceives
the saving Eros by producing magical objects which feed the

fantasy life of the ego and its desire for omnipotence. Art offers itself as 'a mechanism of sensibility which could devour any experience'. (T.S. Eliot on the undissociated sensibility. Plato, perhaps rightly, regards such sensibility as primary in artists.) The separateness, the otherness of art is a sham, a false transcendence, a false imitation of another world. (The negress who sings upon the gramophone record in *La Nausée*.) Art may thus become a magical substitute for philosophy, an impure mediator professing to classify and explain reality. But there is no short cut to enlightenment, and as the *Philebus* (16) tells us, we must sort out the world with patience, not hastily producing a pseudo-unity or *eikon*. Art practises a false degenerate *anamnesis* where the veiled something which is sought and found is no more than a shadow out of the private store-room of the personal unconscious. The work of art may even be thought of as a pernicious caricature of the Form, as the Form was originally conceived, the pure daemonic particular, timeless, radiant, reality-bestowing, separate, directly knowable, and unique.

Plato often makes jokes about his philosophical predecessors in whom the distinction between myth and *logos* is less clearly marked than it is in his own work. An uneasy awareness of the perhaps essential intrusion of (in some sense) myth is no doubt for Plato a part of his old 'quarrel between philosophy and poetry'. Socrates in the *Phaedo* (100 a) says that when he rejected science and turned to *logoi* he was not just using images; and Plato is constantly scrupulous to distinguish clearly between 'pictures' and 'conversations'. However, the artist (or is it the philosopher?) in him still urges him to explain by using images. 'Is it a metaphor?' is of course a fundamental question to be asked about metaphysical explanation, about for instance what we are told in the *Critique of Pure Reason* and the *Phenomenology of Mind*; and indeed such works could not exist at all without the help of metaphor. Plato is right to exclaim (*Timaeus* 47 b) that sight (vision) is our greatest blessing, without which we would not reach philosophy. Our ability to use visual structures to understand non-visual structures (as well as other different visual ones) is fundamental to explanation in any field. The Theory of Forms, when read in conjunction with the explanatory tropes of the Line and the Cave (which may be an Orphic myth colonized by Plato), can certainly produce some blazingly strong imagery in the mind which may well in the long run obstruct understanding. Some of the difficulties of philosophical explanation may be seen in the fact that although Plato at first treats the Forms as quasi-things (what a word means, perfect particulars, 'soul-stuff') and later as attributes, he yet preserves them as objects of divine vision (though we are not told what they 'look like') in the *Timaeus*, because there is something essential that can only be explained by this image. Plato spent some extremely valuable time (*Parmenides*, *Theaetetus*, *Sophist*) dismantling his earlier imagery, but then invented some more, marvellous, entirely new, mythological but still explanatory images in the *Timaeus*. As F. M. Cornford remarks, the Greeks (of Socrates' time) had immense confidence in reason because of advances in geometry. Part of the drama of that confidence was played out in Plato's philosophical life. However, his failures do not lead him (as they might lead a later, Christian or liberal, thinker) to conclude humbly or tolerantly that the human mind is essentially limited and fallible. They lead rather to a firmer sense of hierarchy. Wisdom is *there*, but belongs to gods and very few mortals (*Timaeus*, *Laws*). After all, Plato was continuously involved in politics and even in his middle life was not optimistic about the generality of men. He lived as an active participant through some of the most horrible and harrowing historical events ever recorded in detail, and of which (except in so far as they concerned the death of Socrates) there is almost no direct mention in the dialogues. (The *Theaetetus* opens with the news of Theaetetus, dying of wounds and dysentery after the battle of Corinth, being carried up from the harbour; but the argument then quickly removes us into the past.) Life and (what one must in this context call) art

are here held in a remarkable tension. The dramatic dating
of the dialogues is aesthetically brilliant.

Throughout his work, including the more cheerful earlier
writings, Plato emphasizes the height of the objective and
the difficulty of the ascent. On the other hand, even at his
gloomiest he is never in essentials a sceptic. The Good (truth,
reality) is absent from us and hard of access, but it is there
and only the Good will satisfy. This fact is concealed by the
consoling image-making ego in the guise of the artist whom
every one of us to some extent is. Art with its secret claim
to supreme power blurs the distinction between the presence
and the absence of reality, and tries to cover up with
charming imagery the harsh but inspiring truth of the
distance between man and God. This void may of course also
be concealed by the metaphysical ladders of the philosopher;
it is all very well to tell us to throw away the ladder: the
ladder is interesting. Art, in and out of philosophy, may
ignore the journey and persuade us we are already there and
deny the incommensurabilities of reality and mind. A soften-
ing romanticism dogs philosophy in the guise of art. 'Poetic
pluralism is the corollary to the mysticism of the One' (Edgar
Wind, *Pagan Mysteries of the Renaissance*, 1958, p. 176). But
awareness of the gap is not itself the bridge. Plato knew the
dangers of his own artistry, and the exasperated bitter theological remarks in the *Laws* may express his realization that
as soon as philosophy abandons ψιλοὶ λόγοι, cool unadorned
non-jargon prose, it too is in danger of being used as magic.
The strongest motive to philosophy is probably the same as the
strongest motive to art: the desire to become the Demiurge
and reorganize chaos in accordance with one's own excellent
plan.

Any release of spirit may be ambiguous in its power, and
artists, both visual and literary, love this area of ambiguity,
for reasons well understood by both Plato and Freud. There
has always been a dangerous relationship between art and
religion, and where theology hesitates art will eagerly try
to explain. Art may here be seen as the more 'dangerous'

where 'pure thought' is the less powerful. No wonder (from his own point of view) that Plato, who must by then have felt a diminished faith in the 'high dialectic', kept the artists under such rigid control in the *Laws*, where private speculation is discouraged and picturesque popular religion is an instrument of state power. In fact, unless specifically prevented from doing so, art instinctively materializes God and the religious life. This has been nowhere more true than in Christianity, which has been served by so many genuises. The familiar figures of the Trinity have been so celebrated and beautified in great pictures that it almost seems as if the painters were the final authorities on the matter, as Plato said that the poets seemed to be about the Greek gods. Partly because of the historical nature of Christianity, Christian images tend to be taken 'for real'. Art contributes, in a perhaps misleadingly 'spiritual' way, the material gear of religion; and what should be a mediating agency may become in effect a full-stop barrier. Many modern theologians are attempting to remove this great rigidified and now often unacceptable mythological barrier which divides Christianity from ordinary sophisticated and unsophisticated people. Whether Christian belief can survive this process remains to be seen. Art fascinates religion at a high level and may provide the highest obstacle to the pursuit of the whole truth. A rigid high pattern of integrated 'spiritual' imagery arrests the mind, prevents the free movement of the spirit, and fills the language with unclear metaphor. (The abyss of faith lies beyond images and beyond *logoi* too.) Kierkegaard, as I mentioned earlier, fore-runner of much modern unease about art, sensed these problems and deliberately used art as a destructive anti-theoretical mystification, to promote a more direct relationship to the truth and to prevent the dogmatic relaxation of tension brought about by a hard aesthetically burnished theology. (But art is tricky stuff: did he succeed?)

In the East (an' area so shockingly close to the founders of European rationalism) art is seen as a humbler and more felicitously ambiguous handmaid of religion. Whereas Western art, becoming separated and grand and 'an authority', just as Plato feared, has surreptitiously lent its power to an ossifying of the religion it purports to serve. (The sin of pride.) Although art in the East is even more generally (loosely) connected with religion than it is in the West, the imagery is usually, though significant, less highly specialized, less rationally clarified, less relentlessly literary. The magnificent Hindu deities, however clearly and lovingly rendered, are more mysterious. Eastern religions lack the terrible historical clarity of Christianity. Eastern art is humbler, less 'grand', and has a quieter and perhaps for that reason deeper relation to the spiritual. We may perhaps find a parallel to Plato's attitude in the dignified puritanism of Islam with its reservations about 'figures' and 'objects' and its rejection of role-playing theatre. Zen Buddhists, who are Platonic in their use of the *technai*, but who reject philosophy, actually employ art as anti-art, the favoured images being not only, however skilful, absurdly simple, but also often deliberately incomplete. Many modern visual artists feel an evident sympathy with such attitudes, though they differ about how much skill is required to make anti-art art effective. (This will partly depend of course upon its exact purpose.) Zen also makes use of educational paradoxes (*koan*). Plato's paradoxes (the 'bent' object in water) lead on to measurement, and thus to the cosmic Eros, whereas the paradoxes of Zen are designed to smash rational thought in the interests of a more true and direct understanding. Zen is prepared to use art so long as art does not take itself too seriously; and Zen is well aware of the way in which art imagery may provide false resting places. Pure unpretentious very simple art is the best companion for the religious man. Plato would agree. Zen emphasizes skill but favours throwaway products. Plato (*Laws* 956 b) says that artefacts offered to the gods should be such as can be made in a single day.

Gilbert Ryle describes Plato as an Odysseus rather than a Nestor, and there are of course elements of inconsistency and sheer accident in the work of any persisting thinker. There does, however, seem to be a unity of both thought and feeling in Plato's reactions to art, during the changing pattern of his attitudes to other philosophical questions, and during the momentous history (not discussed here) of his non-philosophical life, including his agonizingly mixed feelings about taking part in politics. That the *Apology* contains an attack on the poets is doubtless significant. *Phaedo* 61 tells how Socrates, although not *mythologikos*, obeyed his dream command to 'make music'. Plato, the heir, so eminently able in this department, puzzled as his master had done about how best to obey. The politically motivated hostility to a free art, which Plato shares with modern dictators, is separable from more refined objections which are both philosophical and temperamental; and although we may want to defend art against Plato's charges we may also recognize, in the context of the highest concern, how worthy of consideration some of these charges are. There is a kind of religious life which excludes art and it is not impossible to understand why.

In fact Plato himself supplies a good deal of the material for a complete aesthetic, a defence and reasonable critique of art. The relation of art to truth and goodness must be the fundamental concern of any serious criticism of it. 'Beauty' cannot be discussed 'by itself'. There is in this sense no 'pure aesthetic' viewpoint. Philosophy and theology have to reject evil in the course of explaining it, but art is essentially more free and enjoys the ambiguity of the whole man; hence the doubleness which of course it shares with Plato's Eros. Where philosophy and theology are purists, art is a shameless collaborator, and Plato rightly identifies irony and laughter as prime methods of collaboration. The judging mind of the skilful artist is a delicate self-effacing instrument; the tone or style by which the writer or painter puts himself 'in the clear' may be very close to a subtle insincerity. (As for instance in what critics call the 'placing' of characters in a novel.) Hence Plato's insight reaches to the deepest levels of our judgement of worth in art. And since his philosophy is largely concerned with how the attractiveness of beauty turns out to be the moral pull of reality, we might expect to be able to extract, in spite of Plato's own negative and often contemptuous attitudes, some positive aesthetic touchstone from his writings. In pursuit of this let us consider for a moment one of his more shocking positions, and one which we might be inclined to dismiss as some sort of 'idle' puritanism: his view of τὸ γελοῖον, the ludicrous or absurd.

Although it may be said in general that philosophy is witty rather than funny and that the same is true of religion (Christ makes witty remarks but not jokes), Plato's work is in fact full of pleasing jokes and is pervaded by a light of humour and sweet-tempered amusement. However, he rejects the ludicrous as πονηρία τις, a kind of vice (*Philebus* 48 c), and says that it signals a lack of self-knowledge. His censor would remove the marvellous description of the gods laughing at the beginning of the *Iliad* (*Iliad* I.599, *Republic* 389 a). The laughter is perhaps not very good-natured, but that is not Plato's point. Laughter (as distinct from amused smiles) is undignified, explosive, something violent and extreme, offending against the modest sobriety which is, with such an impressive backing of theory, commended in the *Philebus*. Of course there is something anti-authoritarian about violent laughter, and there are even today societies, and not primitive ones, where public laughter is frowned upon. The frightened or guilty mind will always wonder: what are they laughing at? Plato more positively, at intervals throughout the dialogues, in the *Republic* as well as in the *Laws*, seems to equate an absurdity-rejecting dignity with some sort of virtuous self-respect. In this he contrasts with his Zen colleagues who (alone of moralists?) take the funny as central to the human pilgrimage. The *koan* often appears as some sort of wild joke. Of course there is a bad absurd (degrading, hurtful), but is there not also a good absurd? Loss of dignity need not be loss of moral stature, can be surrender of vanity, discovery of humility; and a sense of the ludicrous is a

defence against pretensions, not least in art. Plato, however,
in one of the earliest European attempts to define the good
man, as opposed to the hero, attaches importance to his
dignity; and the Judaeo-Christian tradition in general has
shunned presentation of the good man as absurd. (Job is not
absurd.) This may seem natural to us, although it is worth
asking the question whether one can be humble with unimpaired dignity. And of course modern (bourgeois) literature has delighted in the absurd, attractive, good-seeming
hero, a figure whom Plato would no doubt, and perhaps
rightly, view with distaste. Laughter, and the art which
produces it, may notoriously have no *logos*. We laugh wildly
without knowing quite why (lack of self-knowledge) at
situations and absurd jokes which resist analysis. In the
Philebus (65-6) Plato seems to suggest that the absurdity
of sex is repugnant. Freud, discussing jokes (*Jokes and Their
Relation to the Unconscious* iv.2), refers to what he calls the
'fore-pleasure principle' which he also uses in his general
description (already referred to) of the mysterious pleasures
of art. The gentle though often profound jesting of the
dialogues often takes place in situations where love relation-
ships are glanced at, as for instance in the charming picture
of Zeno and Parmenides smiling at each other as they listen
to the youthful Socrates holding forth. These were 'fore-
pleasures' whose possible conclusions the artist Plato keeps
out of view for reasons which closely mingle the aesthetic
and the moral. The dignified tact with which the whole
subject of love is handled is one of the highest effects of
Plato's art.

'Order is beautiful (good), disorder is bad.' The *Republic*
seems to assume a world where what is really real is harmonious, and we can reasonably attempt to know ourselves and
the world. In the *Timaeus* the Demiurge cannot entirely
subdue disorder, and we mortals are victims of 'necessary
passions'. In one of the significant throwaway asides in the
Laws (923 a) the citizens are addressed as 'creatures of a day'
who cannot 'know themselves'. The paradigmatic image of

the clarified world of mathematics, to which the *Republic* gave so high a place, gives way to a more realistic picture of the mind confronting a confused world. The Demiurge is an instructive portrait of the artist in that he is dealing with material which, though endowed with causal properties, is recalcitrant not through being mechanically systematic but through being partly fundamentally jumbled. F. M. Cornford (*Thucydides Mythistoricus*, vol. vi, quoted in his comments on *Timaeus* 47-8) speaks of how Thucydides contrasted the field of ordinary human foresight not with an area of causal law but with an unknown territory of chance full of inscrutable activities of gods and spirits, in the face of which human motives tended to count as absolute beginnings. This, even for us children of a scientific age, is not wholly unlike the way in which we sometimes view the field of our fortunes. The Demiurge has to accept a degree of 'absurdity' (jumble), but he retains the ideal of harmony, and the disorder which faces him is to be deplored, and neither exaggerated nor celebrated.

The discussion in *Philebus* 49-50 connects the ludicrous or absurd with one variety at least of the gleeful envious malice (φθόνος) which Plato associates especially with the theatre, but then extends to 'the whole tragi-comedy of life'. φθόνος is hard to render in English because it contains (as we must understand it in the *Philebus*) an element of sado-masochistic glee which is not fully present in either 'malice' or 'envy'. The narrator of Dostoevsky's *Notes from Underground* (ii.2) both expresses and analyses the concept, as well as providing a loving description of the 'use' of art by the baser mind. 'Everything always finished up to my satisfaction in an entrancingly lazy transition into art, that is into the most delightful forms of existence, all available and ready for me, heartily pinched from poets and novelists, and adaptable to every possible demand and use. For example, I triumph over everybody . . .' etc. The artist, ideally, if he is to proceed beyond the wallpaper stage, should imitate the calm unenvious Demiurge who sees the recalcitrant jumble of his material with just eyes, and with a commanding sense of proportion: that sense of proportion and right order which *Philebus* 16–17 tells us is fostered by dialectic. But Plato will not allow that this is possible. The bad artist (who resides in all of us) as naive fantasist, to use the distinction of the *Sophist* and the imagery of the Cave, sees only moving shadows and construes the world in accordance with the easy unresisted mechanical 'causality' of his personal dream-life. (The bad thriller or facile romance and its client.) The mediocre artist (the ironical man by the fire, if we may so characterize him), who thinks he 'knows himself but too well', parades his mockery and spleen as a despairing dramatic rejection of any serious or just attempt to discern real order at all. This figure (a fairly familiar one in the pages of Plato's dialogues, where he is criticized, and of modern literature, where he is indulged) is on the road toward the 'all is permitted' and 'man is the measure of all things' of the cynical sophist. Neither of these, as artist or as man, possesses true self-knowledge or a just grasp of the hardness of the material which resists him, the necessity, the ἀνάγκη of the world. Confronted with semi-chaos the Demiurge is steadied (if he needs it) by the presence of the Forms. But must the mortal artist, condemned to some variety of self-indulgence, be either a dreamer or a cynic; and can he not attempt to see the created world in the pure light of the Forms?

It is tempting to 'refute' Plato simply by pointing to the existence of great works of art, and in doing so to describe their genesis and their merits in Platonic terms. Kant, though suspicious of beauty because of its possible lapse into charm, was prepared to treat it as a symbol of the good (*Critique of Judgement* i.59); and could not art at least be so regarded, even if we take Plato's objections seriously? Good art, thought of as symbolic force rather than statement, provides a stirring image of a pure transcendent value, a steady visible enduring higher good, and perhaps provides for many people, in an unreligious age without prayer or sacraments, their clearest *experience* of something grasped as separate and precious and beneficial and held quietly and unpossessively in the attention. Good art which we love can seem holy and attending to it can be like praying. Our relation to such art though 'probably never' entirely pure is markedly unselfish. The calm joy in the picture gallery is quite unlike the pleasurable flutter felt in the sale room. Beauty is, as Plato says, visibly transcendent; hence indeed the metaphor of vision so indispensable in discussions of aesthetics and morality. The *spectacle* of good in other forms, as when we admire good men and heroes, is often, as experience, more mixed and less efficacious. As Kierkegaard said, we admire and relax. Good art, on the other hand, provides work for the spirit. Of course morality is quite largely a matter of action, though what we look at profoundly affects what we do. ('Whatsoever things are honest . . . whatsoever things are pure . . . think on these things.' Philippians 4:8.) And of course the practice of personal relations is the fundamental school of virtue. The spiritual revelations involved in dealing with people are in an evident sense more important than those available through art, though they tend to be less clear. What are motives and do they matter? When is altruism an exercise of power? (etc. etc. etc.) Of course such questions need, in particular cases, answers. But art remains available and vivid as an experience of how egoism can be purified by intelligent imagination. Art-beauty must in a sense be detached from good because art is not essential. Art, though it demands moral effort and teaches quiet attention (as any serious study can do) is a kind of treat; it is, like Kant's Sublime, an extra. We can be saved without seeing the Alps or the Cairngorms, and without Titian and Mozart too. We have to make moral choices, we do not have to enjoy great art and doubtless many good people never do. But surely great art points in the direction of the good and is at least more valuable to the moralist as an auxiliary than dangerous as an enemy. How, when, whether bad art (of which of course there is a great deal) is morally damaging is, as we know, a deep question not easily answered. For great art to exist a general practice of art must exist; and even trivial art is a fairly harmless consolation, as Plato himself seems prepared to admit in the *Laws*.

Of course art is huge, and European philosophy is strangely small, so that Whitehead scarcely exaggerates in calling it all footnotes to Plato. General talk about 'art', to which one is driven when discussing Plato's view, is always in danger of becoming nonsense. There is no science of criticism; any so-called critical 'system' has in the end to be evaluated by the final best instrument, the calm open judging mind of the intelligent experienced critic, unmisted, as far as possible, by theory. Confronted with academic aesthetics as he knew it, Tolstoy's instincts were sound, and his reply to the effect that all we need to know is that good art promotes good, is one with which we can sympathize. However one is tempted, and partly in order to do justice to Plato's argument, to try to explain in more detail just how great art is good for us, and in doing so to take our best material out of Plato himself. Art is a special discerning exercise of intelligence in relation to the real; and although aesthetic form has essential elements of trickery and magic, yet form in art, as form in philosophy, is designed to communicate and reveal. In the shock of joy in response to good art, an essential ingredient is a sense of the revelation of reality, of the really real, the ὄντως ὄν: the world as we were never able so clearly to see it before. When Burne-Jones is reported as saying 'I mean by a picture a beautiful romantic dream of something that never was, never will be—in a light better than any light that ever shone—in a land no one can define or remember, only desire—and the forms divinely beautiful', we are embarrassed, not least because this does indeed seem to describe many of his pictures in an aspect which marks them as delightful or marvellous but not exactly great. (See F. de Lisle, *Burne-Jones*, 1904, p. 173, quoted by John Christian in Hayward Gallery Burne-Jones Exhibition Catalogue 1975.) One would not think of applying such language to the work of (for instance) Seurat or Cézanne, or to remoter and apparently 'fanciful' art, such as mythological subjects treated by Botticelli or Titian. When Artemis speeds by as Actaeon falls, the revelation remains mysterious but somehow true, and with the 'hardness' of truth. A reading of Plato helps us to see how good art is truthful. Dream is the enemy of art and its false image. As pictured in the *Republic*, the higher level is reflected as an image in the lower level. The high-temperature fusing power of the creative imagination, so often and eloquently described by the Romantics, is the reward of the sober truthful mind which, as it reflects and searches, constantly says no and no and no to the prompt easy visions of self-protective self-promoting fantasy. (Like the daemon of Socrates which said only 'No.') The artist's 'freedom' is hard won, and is a function of his grasp of reality. To adapt Plato's image, the Demiurge creates time as an, interestingly transformed, image of eternity, but finds the mysterious essential medium of space already existing. The images which body forth the truth come spontaneously, in the end, into the space which it is so hard to apprehend and accept, and to keep empty against the pressures which are tending to collapse it. (The *Vorlust* is always impatient for a conclusion.) The imagination fuses, but in order to do so it must tease apart in thought what is apart in reality, resisting the facile merging tendencies of the obsessive ego. The prescription for art is then the same as for dialectic: overcome personal fantasy and egoistic anxiety and self-indulgent day-dream. Order and separate and distinguish the world justly. Magic in its unregenerate form as the fantastic doctoring of the real for consumption by the private ego is the bane of art as it is of philosophy. Obsession shrinks reality to a single pattern. The artist's worst enemy is his eternal companion, the cosy dreaming ego, the dweller in the vaults of *eikasia*. Of course the highest art is powered by the force of an individual unconscious mind, but then so is the highest philosophy; and in both cases technique is useless without divine fury.

What is hard and necessary and unavoidable in human fate is the subject-matter of great art. To use a mixture of Platonic and Kantian language, we see in a dream that art is properly concerned with the synthetic *a priori*, the borderland of *dianoia* and *noesis*, the highest mental states described in the *Republic*. Art is about the pilgrimage from appearance to reality (the subject of every good play and novel) and exemplifies in spite of Plato what his philosophy teaches concerning the therapy of the soul. This is the 'universal', the high concern which Tolstoy said was the proper province of the artist. The divine (intelligent) cause persuades the necessary cause so as to bring about the best possible. It is the task of mortals (as artists and as men) to understand the necessary for the sake of the intelligible, to see in a pure just light the hardness of the real properties of the world, the effects of the wandering causes, why good purposes are checked and where the mystery of the random has to be accepted. It is not easy to do justice to this hardness and this randomness without either smoothing them over with fantasy or exaggerating them into (cynical) absurdity. Indeed 'the absurd' in art, often emerging as an attempt to defeat easy fantasy, may merely provide it with a sophisticated disguise. The great artist, while showing us what is not saved, implicitly shows us what salvation means. Of course the Demiurge is attempting against insuperable difficulties to create a harmonious and just world. The (good) human artist, whom Plato regards as such a base caricature, is trying to portray the partially failed world as it is, and in doing so to produce something pleasing and beautiful. This involves an intelligent disciplined understanding of what may be called the structural problems of the Demiurge. There is a 'sublime absurd', comic or tragic, which depends on this insight into where the 'faults' come. (Both *2 Henry IV* III.ii and *King Lear* V.iii.) Forgivably or unforgivably, there is a partly intelligible causality of sin. The good artist helps us to see the place of necessity in human life, what must be endured, what makes and breaks, and to purify our imagination so as to contemplate the real world (usually veiled by anxiety and fantasy) including what is terrible and absurd. Plato said at *Republic* 395 a that no one

can write both comedy and tragedy. As the *Symposium* ends
Socrates is telling Agathon and Aristophanes that this can be
done. One would like to have an account of this conversation. Plato, with a perverse negligence, never favours us with
any serious literary criticism.

Moral philosophers, attempting to analyse human frailty,
have produced some pretty unrealistic schemata, usually because they were trying to do too many things at the same
time. The contemporary philosopher is in this respect more
modest. The question, at what level of generality am I to
operate? is of course one which faces both the artist and the
philosopher. Great discoveries are made at great levels of
generality, as when Plato subjects the profound idea that no
one errs willingly to a number of transformations within a
general picture of the human soul as knower and agent. On
the other hand, the lack of detail can leave the reader uncon-
vinced that he is really seeing 'human life' and not the
'ghostly ballet of bloodless categories', the vision of which
haunted another and more recent Platonist, F.H. Bradley.
To take one example, Plato, wishing to make the different
levels of the soul correspond to different tasks in society and
different types of state, connects his concept of θυμοειδές,
the central transformational region of the soul, especially
with honour and ambition, and thereby oversimplifies a concept which is essential to his analysis of moral change. The
Republic, like many other great ethical treatises, is deficient
in an account of positive evil. The 'tyrannical man' has to
prove too much. A portrayal of moral reflection and moral
change (degeneration, improvement) is the most important
part of any system of ethics. The explanation of our fallibi-
lity in such matters as seeing the worse as the better is more
informatively (though of course less systematically) carried
out by poets, playwrights, and novelists. It has taken philosophy a long time to acknowledge this: the famous 'quarrel'
is indeed of long standing, and the suspicion that art is fundamentally frivolous. It is only comparatively recently that
moral philosophers have condescended to enlist the

aid of literature as a mode of explanation.

The sight of evil is confusing, and it is a subject on which it is hard to generalize because any analysis demands such a battery of value judgements. One would like to think that the just man sees the unjust man clearly. ('God sees him clearly.') Art is (often too) jauntily at home with evil and quick to beautify it. Arguably however, good literature is uniquely able publicly to clarify evil, and emulate the just man's private vision without, such is his privilege, the artist having to be just except in his art. That this separation is possible seems a fact of experience. Art accepts and enjoys the ambiguity of the whole man, and great artists can seem to 'use' their own vices for creative purposes without apparent damage to their art. This mystery belongs indeed to the region of the unmeasured and unlimited. Plato understands what criticism must be constantly aware of, how the bad side of human nature is secretly, precariously, at work in art. There is a lot of secret cruelty there and if the art is good enough (consider Dante, or Dostoevsky) it may be hard to decide when the disciplined 'indulgence' of the cruelty damages the merit of the work or harms the client. But to see misery and evil justly is one of the heights of aesthetic endeavour and one which is surely sometimes reached. How this becomes beautiful is a mystery which may seem very close to some of the central and most lively obscurities in Plato's own thought. (The divine cause is always touching the necessary cause.) Shakespeare makes not only splendour but beauty out of the malevolence of Iago and the intolerable death of Cordelia, as Homer does out of the miseries of a pointless war and the stylish ruthlessness of Achilles. Art can rarely, but with authority, show how we learn from pain, swept by the violence of divine grace toward an unwilling wisdom, as described in the first chorus of the *Agamemnon* in words which somehow remind us of Plato, who remained (it appears) so scandalously indifferent to the merits of Aeschylus. (A case of envy?) And of course art can reveal without explaining and its justice can also be playful.

The docility of necessity to intelligence may be as vividly evident in non-mimetic non-conceptual art ('pure contraption' and 'absolute gift'), which fleetingly illuminates deep structures of reality, as if the artist could indeed penetrate the creative reverie of the Demiurge where truth and play mysteriously, inextricably mingle.

One might, in praising art to Plato, even add that if there is, as an effective persuasion, an ontological proof (Plato's main idea after all), art provides a very plausible version of it. Perhaps in general art *proves* more than philosophy can. Familiarity with an art form and the development of taste is an education in the beautiful which involves the often largely instinctive, increasingly confident sorting out of what is good, what is pure, what is profoundly and justly imagined, what rings true, from what is trivial or shallow or in some way fake, self-indulgent, pretentious, sentimental, meretriciously obscure, and so on. Most derogatory critical terms impute some kind of falsehood, and on the other hand (Keats) 'what the imagination seizes as beauty must be truth'. Bad art is a lie about the world, and what is by contrast seen as good is in some important evident sense seen as *ipso facto* true and as expressive of reality: the sense in which Seurat is better than Burne-Jones, Keats than Swinburne, Dickens than Wilkie Collins, etc. etc. Plato says in the *Philebus* that an experience of pleasure may be infected with falsity. Learning to detect the false in art and enjoy the true is part of a life-long education in moral discernment. This does not mean living in an aesthetic cloister. Good art, however complex, presents an evident combination of purity and realism: and if we think at once of moral teachings which do the same (the Gospels, St. Augustine, Julian of Norwich, parts of Plato), it has to be admitted that these too are in their own perfectly natural way art. The development of any skill increases our sense of (necessity) reality. Learning an art is learning all sorts of strange tricks, but fundamentally it is learning how to make a formal utterance of a perceived truth and render it splendidly worthy of a trained purified

attention without falsifying it in the process. When Plato
says (*Philebus* 48 d) that to enjoy the ridiculous is to obey
the command: do not know thyself, he is using (though
perversely) an important principle of literary criticism: that
which militates against self-knowledge is suspect. To know
oneself *in the world* (as part of it, subject to it, connected
with it) is to have the firmest grasp of the real. This is the
humble 'sense of proportion' which Plato connects with
virtue. Strong agile realism, which is of course not photo-
graphic naturalism, the non-sentimental, non-meanly-personal
imaginative grasp of the subject-matter is something which
can be recognized as value in all the arts, and it is this which
gives that special unillusioned pleasure which is the liberating
whiff of reality; when in high free play the clarified imaginative attention of the creative mind is fixed upon its object.
Of course art is playful, but its play is serious. τῆς σπουδῆς
ἀδελφὴ παιδιά. Freud says that the opposite of play is not
work but reality. This may be true of fantasy play but not
of the playfulness of good art which delightedly seeks and
reveals the real. Thus in practice we increasingly relate one
concept to another, and see beauty as the artful use of form
to illuminate truth, and celebrate reality; and we can then
experience what Plato spoke of but wished to separate from
art: the way in which to desire the beautiful is to desire the
real and the good.

It may be tempting here to say that the disciplined understanding, the just discernment, of the good artist must
depend (if one wants to play further with the *Timaeus* myth)
upon some kind of *separate* moral certainty. Again the metaphor of vision: a source of light. However it is difficult to
press the idea beyond the status of a tautology. Good artists
can be bad men; the virtue may, as I said earlier, reside entirely in the work, the just vision be attainable only there.
After all, however much we idolize each other, we are limited
specialized animals. Moreover, even the work itself may be
less perfect than it seems. We are creatures of a day, nothing
much. We do not understand ourselves, we lack reality, what

we have and know is not ὄντως ὄν, but merely ὄν πῶς. We
are cast in the roles of Shallow and Silence; and must not, in
favour of art or philosophy, protest too much. (The best in
this kind are but shadows, and the worst are no worse, if
imagination amend them.) Because of the instinctive com-
pleting activity of the client's mind, its 'unlimited' co-
operation with the artist, we often do not see how unfinished
even great work may be; and if the artist presses this upon
our attention we are shocked since we so much want to
believe in perfection. Great works of art often do seem like
perfect particulars, and we seem here to enjoy that 'extra'
knowledge which is denied to us at the end of the *Theaetetus*.
But because of the muddle of human life and the ambiguity
and playfulness of aesthetic form, art can at best only explain
partly, only reveal almost; and of course any complex work
contains impurities and accidents which we choose to ignore.
Even the Demiurge will never entirely understand. Although
art can be so good for us, it does contain some of those
elements of illusion out of which its detractors make so much
of their case. The pierced structure of the art object whereby
its sense flows into life is an essential part of its mortal
nature. Even at its most exquisite art is incomplete. Simone
Weil, that admirable Platonist, said that a poem is beautiful
in so far as the poet's thought is fixed upon the ineffable.
Art, like (in Plato's view) philosophy, hovers about in the
very fine air which we breathe just beyond what has been
expressed.

One need not, however, enter into metaphysical or psychological arguments to diminish art or to defend it either. Its
simpler solider merits are obvious: a free art is an essential
aspect of a free society, as a degraded lying art is a function
of a tyrannical one. Art as the great general universal informant is an obvious rival, not necessarily a hostile one, to
philosophy and indeed to science, and Plato never did justice
to the unique truth-conveying capacities of art. The good or
even decent writer does not just 'imitate doctors' talk', but
attempts to understand and portray the doctors' 'world', and

these pictures, however modest, of other 'worlds' are interesting and valuable. The spiritual ambiguity of art, its connection with the 'limitless' unconscious, its use of irony, its interest in evil, worried Plato. But the very ambiguity and voracious ubiquitousness of art is its characteristic freedom. Art, especially literature, is a great hall of reflection where we can all meet and where everything under the sun can be examined and considered. For this reason it is feared and attacked by dictators, and by authoritarian moralists such as the one under discussion. The artist is a great informant, at least a gossip, at best a sage, and much loved in both roles. He lends to the elusive particular a local habitation and a name. He sets the world in order and gives us hypothetical hierarchies and intermediate images: like the dialectician he mediates between the one and the many; and though he may artfully confuse us, on the whole he instructs us. Art is far and away the most educational thing we have, far more so than its rivals, philosophy and theology and science. The pierced nature of the work of art, its limitless connection with ordinary life, even its defencelessness against its client, are part of its characteristic availability and freedom. The demands of science and philosophy and ultimately of religion are extremely rigorous. It is just as well that there is a high substitute for the spiritual and the speculative life: that few get to the top morally or intellectually is no less than the truth. Art is a great international human language, it is for all. Of course art has no formal 'social role' and artists ought not to feel that they must 'serve their society'. They will automatically serve it if they attend to truth and try to produce the best art (make the most beautiful things) of which they are capable. The connection of truth with beauty means that art which succeeds in being for itself also succeeds in being for everybody. And even without the guarantee of a Platonic aesthetic, art need not be too humble. Hear the words of Jane Austen (*Northanger Abbey*, Chapter V). '"And what are you reading Miss——?" "Oh, it is only a novel", replies the young lady; while she lays down her book with affected indifference, or momentary shame.—"It is only Cecilia, or Camilla, or Belinda"; or, in short, only some work in which the greatest powers of the mind are displayed, in which the most thorough knowledge of human nature, the happiest delineation of its varieties, the liveliest effusion of wit and humour are conveyed to the world in the best chosen language.'

The most obvious paradox in the problem under consideration is that Plato is a great artist. It is not perhaps to be imagined that the paradox troubled him too much. Scholars in the land of posterity assemble the work and invent the problems. Plato had other troubles, many of them political. He fought a long battle against sophistry and magic, yet produced some of the most memorable images in European philosophy: the Cave, the charioteer, the cunning homeless Eros, the Demiurge cutting the *Anima Mundi* into strips and stretching it out crosswise. He kept emphasizing the imageless remoteness of the Good, yet kept returning in his exposition to the most elaborate uses of art. The dialogue form itself is artful and indirect and abounds in ironical and playful devices. Of course the statements made by art escape into the free ambiguity of human life. Art cheats the religious vocation at the last moment and is inimical to philosophical categories. Yet neither philosophy nor theology can do without it; there has to be a pact between them, like the pact in the *Philebus* between reason and pleasure.

Plato says (*Phaedrus*, Letter VIII) that no sensible man will commit his thought to words and that a man's thoughts are likely to be better than his writings. Without raising philosophical problems about what a man's thoughts *are*, one may reply that the discipline of committing oneself to clarified public form is proper and rewarding: the final and best discoveries are often made in the actual formulation of the statement. The careful responsible skilful use of words is our highest instrument of thought and one of our highest modes of being: an idea which might seem obvious but is not now by any means universally accepted. There may in theoretical studies, as in art, be so-called ultra-verbal insights at any level; but to call ultimate truth ineffable is to utter a quasi-religious principle which should not be turned round against the careful verbalization of humbler truths. Nor did Plato in practice do this. He wanted what he more than once mentions, immortality through art; he felt and indulged the artist's desire to produce unified, separable, formal, durable objects. He was also the master, indeed, the inventor, of a pure calm relaxed mode of philosophical exposition which is a high literary form and a model forever. Of course he used metaphor, but philosophy needs metaphor and metaphor is basic; how basic is the most basic philosophical question. Plato also had no doubt a strong personal motive which prompted him to write. Socrates (*Theaetetus* 210 c) called himself a barren midwife. Plato often uses images of paternity. Art launches philosophy as it launches religion, and it was necessary for Plato, as it was for the evangelists, to write if the Word was not to be sterile and the issue of the Father was to be recognized as legitimate.

Plato feared the consolations of art. He did not offer a consoling theology. His psychological realism depicted God as subjecting mankind to a judgement as relentless as that of the old Zeus, although more just. A finely meshed moral causality determines the fate of the soul. That the movement of the saving of Eros is toward an impersonal pictureless void is one of the paradoxes of a complete religion. To present the idea of God at all, even as myth, is a consolation, since it is impossible to defend this image against the prettifying attentions of art. Art will mediate and adorn, and develop magical structures to conceal the absence of God or his distance. We live now amid the collapse of many such structures, and as religion and metaphysics in the West withdraw from the embraces of art, we are it might seem being forced to become mystics through the lack of any imagery which could satisfy the mind. Sophistry and magic break down at intervals, but they never go away and there is no end to their collusion with art and to the consolations which, perhaps fortunately for the human race, they can provide; and art, like writing and like Eros, goes on existing for better and for worse.